Victoriana Americana

by Evelyn Swenson

Greatlakes Living Press, Publishers, Matteson, Illinois

Victoriana Americana
©Evelyn Swenson 1976
All rights reserved
Printed in the U.S.A.
ISBN: 0-915498-31-6
Library of Congress Catalog Number: 76-16736

Cover design by Joseph Mistak, Jr.
Cover photograph by Patrick K. Snook and Jerry Trehan
Other design by Chris Avers

Greatlakes Living Press
3634 W. 216th Street
Matteson, Illinois 60443

Contents

Preface

Dozens of books and thousands of words have been written about the great gems of the world and the famous people who owned and wore them. That little has been written about black glass jewelry is not surprising. Essentially it was cheaper jewelry, made for the masses, and certainly not very newsworthy. The story of the Hope diamond is far more exciting than a black glass cameo worn by a little grayhaired old lady.

Inquiries to museums across the country, and to England, brought little factual information. A year of research, digging in some very unlikely places, brought together strange little bits and pieces, which when finally assembled began to tell a story. And a most curious story it proved to be—how the jet craze came to America, and how the influence of one man, reaching across the ocean from the continent of Europe, helped to create the craze. It also is a story that could have happened only in Victorian America—the time and the climate were just right.

The word "jet," as used in this book, refers basically to black glass, since jet became the generic term for old black glass jewelry and its twin sister, the beautiful black passementerie beadwork. Some of the statements made herein are based on guesswork; for any wrong guesses made, please accept them as honest errors of interpretation.

Evelyn Swenson

October, 1976

Acknowledgments

For a hobby to grow and blossom, the help and encouragement of others are necessary ingredients. During two years of research my cup did indeed "runneth over." A very large debt is owed to Mrs. Doris Colby, head librarian, and her very capable staff of the Aurora College Library in Aurora, Illinois. Access was allowed to old archives, with staff members combing out the "oldies but goodies," so valuable in the research process. The staff of the Aurora Public Library were equally gracious in lending their assistance.

Aurora College faculty members, Dr. Gerald Roehrig, professor of chemistry and chairman of the science division; Dr. Steven Hannum, associate professor of the science division; and Paul Sipiera, instructor in geology, were most helpful in conducting tests (among them the X-Ray Defraction test) on the odd bits of material that wandered into my hands.

The Aurora Historical Society, Mr. Fred Graham, president; and Mrs. Judy Hankes, assistant curator, are thanked especially for their permission to use the Carriage House (on the back cover) and for assisting in the photographing of the true jet necklace.

To Mr. Norbert Gengler, a very special tribute for his untiring patience during the long photography sessions. Black glass is a most difficult subject to photograph since the deepness of the color and the high reflections tend to produce distortions and drink up the spotlighting.

Mauriceline (Marcy) F. Reed executed the designs of the small buttons and the sketches from the pages of the *Ladies Home Journal*. Marcy is a senior student at Aurora College, combining her talents both in the artistic field and in the Criminal Justice Program. Thank you, Marcy.

The author expresses her appreciation to Mr. Robert V. Hull, head of adult services of the Leominster Public Library for the loan of *Comb Making in America*, compiled and privately published for Bernard W. Doyle, president of the Viscoloid Company, Inc., 1925. To the best of my knowledge, this publication contains one of the most complete detailings of the rise of the horn industry in America. Mr. Doyle pioneered in the introduction of celluloid into the comb making industry, naming the product developed from celluloid, "Viscoloid."

Special thanks to Curtis Publishing Company for permission to use material from the *Ladies' Home Journal* on the early history of the founding of the House of Worth. (Downe Publishing Co., Inc., owns the *Ladies' Home Journal* and all its copyrights, but those in the earlier years still are listed under Curtis Publishing).

A special thank you to Mrs. John Gearhart, III, for her letter (quoted in chapter 4) and her help in tracking down the photo of Miss Nancy Dawson; and to W. Porter Ware, for the loan of the Jenny Lind photos in chapter 2.

To the many curators of museums across the country who took the time to answer my letters of inquiry, a special thank you.

Acknowledgment is made to the many publishing houses who graciously permitted the use of their works in direct quotation or reference.

Others who made special contributions are indicated within the text; without their help, portions of this book would not have been possible.

For
Beth and Lorri

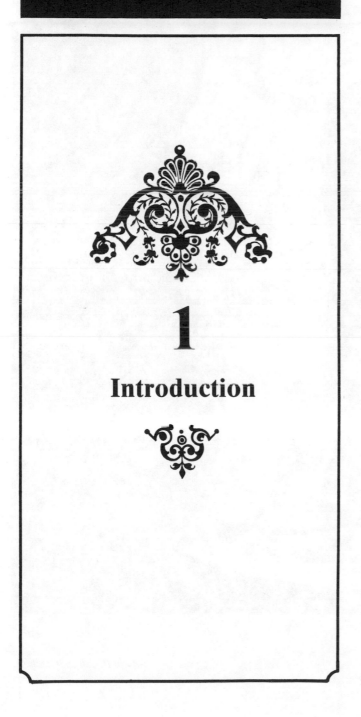

THE WAY IT WAS

1

Introduction

For most 20th Century Americans, the word "Victorianism" conjures up visions of horsehair sofas, gee-gaws, jimcracks and gingerbread. While the Victorian era certainly contained all of these elements and more, the 19th Century in America was a period of dynamic growth that literally exploded the nation from coast to coast.

As the new nation struggled to become a reality, post-revolutionary America was characterized by slavery, dueling, hanging for petty theft, public whipping, wife beating and child selling. Although the apron strings had been cut, the people of the New World still harbored strong ties and loyalties to England. Most magazines and books were still imported; American editors, armed with scissors and a big paste pot, simply transferred much of the printed matter from English publications to their own. The grumblings of the English were echoed in the New World, along with American complaints.

The rule of the Georges had done little to build the confidence of the English people. The Royal House of England blithely assumed it could do no wrong, and went merrily on its way. George III (1738-1820), often derisively called "Farmer George" and "The Royal Buttonmaker," did not hesitate to use corruption to put his political theories into practice. In the later years of his life, blindness and the immoral conduct of his son, the Prince of Wales, embittered his life. The prince finally succeeded in driving his father hopelessly insane, and succeeded to the throne as George IV (1762-1830).

Nicknamed "Prinny," George IV possessed a foul temper and a tremendous capacity to spend money as if it were going out of style. Money was no object when he commissioned the construction of the Pavilion at Brighton, the first building of Oriental influence to be erected in England. Prinny's death in 1830 brought William IV (1765-1837) to the throne, a King who was utterly incapable of understanding anything, much less of thinking anything through. The English people dubbed him "Silly Billy." Exercising his royal prerogatives, he lived for many years with a Mrs. Jordan, an actress, by whom he had a family of five sons and five daughters. Evidently, Silly Billy did understand a few things. Fortunately, government by the Ministry was well developed, and William's mental instability did little harm. Even more fortunate was the shortness of his reign (1830-1837). His death in 1837 brought to the throne Alexandrina Victoria, only daughter and child of Edward, Duke of Kent, fourth son of George III.

1

Edwin Booth as Richilieu.

While the English people complained about Prinny and Silly Billy, the American people witnessed a savage political campaign waged against Andrew Jackson. Jackson's liberal money policy in 1834 brought financial crisis that resulted in banks closing and businessmen forced into bankruptcy. Inflation hit hard, riots occurred and, by 1837, thousands of businesses had closed their doors. Both England and America were ready for a change.

Lord John Russell, an able orator and excellent psychologist, became Victoria's press agent. His was the task of selling not only the English people, but the world, the greatness of the new queen. He extolled the queen's virtues over and over: She was good, she was religious, she was pure, her life was dedicated to becoming virtue's own reward; let all people follow the young queen in rules of good conduct. The soft voice in America that echoed Lord Russell's message belonged to Sarah Josepha Hale, who had just become the first female editor in America. For the next 40 years, Sarah Hale was to be the foremost spokesman for and to women of America. A deeply religious and patriotic woman, Sarah hailed goodness and virtue throughout her long career. And poor Victoria never knew how good she would have to be until she married stiff-necked Albert.

As Victoria began her reign, New York was still a country bumpkin village with wooden water pumps set every four blocks and pigs acting as garbage collectors. Chicago was a desolate, wild-onion swamp marked with cattails, high coarse grass and bullfrogs, with its few citizens living nearby in shanties and cabins. Beyond Chicago lay the vast western territories—a sleeping giant. During the next 60 years, America was transformed from an agricultural society into a highly industrialized nation. In rapid succession came the sewing machine, telegraph, telephone, transcontinental railroads, steamships and electricity. Issues of the *Scientific American* between 1850 and 1890 are an amazing chronicle of the inventiveness of the Yankee mind, producing everything from the simplest household gadget to complex machinery, tunnels and bridges.

In the amazing kaleidoscope that was Victoriana, chivalry, sentimentality, piety, prudery, brutality, quackery and oratory joined hands and marched together. Individual fortunes reached astronomical proportions and the resulting power they placed in the hands of a few nearly ruined the country. War, graft, chicanery, double dealing and wholesale corruption invaded the White House itself. We may scoff at the Victorian modes and manners, yet these Victorians succeeded in creating the American style—wholly our own—whether for good or bad being a matter of individual opinion. As a people, they were no better and no worse than those who have walked before and after them.

Of all the many phenomena to surface, none was more striking than the religious movements that spread across 19th Century America. Some movements were founded by sincere, honest people, others by charlatans who used religion as their personal road to prestige and wealth.

The rise of the Mormons began in the 1820s with the visions of Joseph Smith in New York state. Suspicion, hostility and outright violence walked with them along their trail from New York to Utah, where they finally settled in 1850, with Brigham Young appointed governor of the Utah territory. In the 1830s, Rev. William Miller, "The Prophet," earnestly preached the end of the world, which his followers decided would occur in 1843. Unlike the Mormons, the followers of Rev. Miller found only ridicule and scorn when the long-awaited event did not occur.

The Oneida Community Plate had its start in 1848 in the person of John Humphrey Noyes, who began the colony as a "free love" society. During the period known as the "Great Awakening" (1857-1858), churches were crowded daily; the largest public places and theaters were used as meeting halls. There were no central figures or leaders in the movement, and those who attended the prayer meetings came from every walk of life, representing many faiths.

Another period of religious revival occured in 1875, spearheaded by Dwight L. Moody and Ira D. Sankey, lay evangelists. Appearing before crowds of thousands in Brooklyn and Philadelphia, touring through the South and the West, Moody's impassioned preaching and Sankey's singing filled the halls wherever they went.

The theater was as much a hallmark of Victoriana as religion. As the small towns sprang up, each boasted of its church, opera house and saloons (alcoholism became a very serious problem). Small troupes of actors toured the country—by wagon, stagecoach, canal barge, horseback, mule, boat, railroad and on foot. Their endurance should have earned them gold medals for they suffered all the dangers of travel—bad food, poor lodgings, inadequate theaters—and often earned little money. Staying clean was a never-ending battle and no actor ventured forth on tour without a generous supply of Fuller's earth to sprinkle on his clothing to absorb dirt and grease. One unwritten law of the troupers was to avoid appearing in a town at the same time a religious camp meeting was in progress. The two just didn't mix very well!

Across the stages of America came Cordelia Howard, the original Little Eva of *Uncle Tom's Cabin*; Tyrone

FORREST ALS METAMORA.

Edwin Booth as Metamora

Power, great-grandfather of the movie star of the 1940s; James O'Neill, father of playwright Eugene O'Neill; Edwin Booth, brother of John Wilkes Booth; Edwin Forrest, creating the role of Metamora, one of the first plays to be written about American Indians; Charlotte (Lotta) Crabtree; the Drew Dynasty that was eventually to produce the illustrious Barrymores—Lionel, Ethel and John; and the most glamorous gal of all—Lillian Russell, the American Beauty, upon whom Diamond Jim Brady showered his little diamond doo-dads.

It didn't take long for European artists to catch on that there might be gold in "them thar hills." Beautiful Fanny Kemble of England was one of the first to try her luck in the New World in 1832, touring New York, Philadelphia, Boston, Washington, Quebec and Montreal. The Prince of Humbugs, P.T. Barnum, set America on its ear by persuading Jenny Lind, the Swedish Nightingale, to come to America for a concert tour. Using every trick in the book, and probably inventing a few new ones, P.T. built the anticipation of the American public to a fever pitch. How well he succeeded is documented by the fact that 50 years later the old-timers still talked about the time "when Jenny Lind sang."

Another to hit the golden trail to America was Sarah Bernhardt of France, the leading actress of Europe, a title with which she always agreed. During her lifetime she made a fortune, promptly spent twice as much, and always was on the ragged edge of bankruptcy. Edward Jarret borrowed P.T. Barnum's bag of tricks when he brought Sarah to America in 1880. She became a sensation overnight, with her every move reported in the newspapers. Sarah could in rapid succession, be capricious, willful, obstinate, charming, lovable, mean, hateful and, on occasion, downright catty. Her personal life was a banquet feast for the scandal mongers, yet she lived life to its fullest—even in the midst of Victorian prudery and piety—with supreme disregard for the opinion of others. America became Sarah's personal gold mine. Whenever she needed money, which was most of the time, another tour of America was made, even in her later years of life when she had only one leg.

Another remarkable woman who left her stamp on Victoriana was the beautiful Jersey Lily—Lily Langtry, daughter of Rev. W.C. Le Breton, dean of Jersey, a small island off the coast of England. "Lily Langtry," said John Everett Millais, "happens to be, quite simply, the most beautiful woman on earth." Like Sarah, Lily was gossiped about, written about, talked about, photographed; her name was linked with dozens of men. She, too, made a fortune but, unlike Sarah, Lily was a very sane and sensible businesswoman. Careful investments

Sarah Bernhardt theater program (L'Aiglon), c. 1900s.

Lily Langtry

and cautious buying and selling in real estate eventually made her a millionaire.

These and many more were to grace the stages of America—Henry Irving, Ellen Terry, Helen Modjeska, Yvette Guilbert, Mrs. Patric Campbell, and the great prima donna, Adelina Patti.

Out of the melting pot that was America came the men who were to amass fortunes that still boggle the mind today. In the late 1700s, John Jacob Astor I made the greatest single American fortune; beginning first in the fur trade, Astor then went into the china trade and finally settled in real estate. By the simple act of buying land and then sitting on it, Astor became tremendously wealthy. His son, William, added to the family fortunes during the New York Panic of 1837. August Belmont, the American representative of the Rothschilds, also profited by the panic. Picking up real estate, Belmont did so well he was able to open his own investment house in 1838. Commodore Vanderbilt laid the foundation of his fortune in shipping as early as 1818. A.T. Stewart, a Belfast immigrant, opened his department store in New York in 1825, and eventually earned the title of the "Merchant Prince." In the face of the 1837 panic two enterprising young men opened a small store just south of A.T. Stewart with an assorted line of goods. John P. Young and Charles L. Tiffany felt the worst that could happen would be that they might not succeed, in which case each would simply return to his family business.

By 1850, Chicago had evolved into a town of dirt streets and plank sidewalks. Fleets of ships unloaded produce and merchandise daily; railroads were hauling wheat into the town. Into this setting walked Cyrus T. McCormick, Philip Danforth Armour, Potter Palmer, Levi Leiter, Marshall Field, Aaron Montgomery Ward, George Pullman, Martin Ryerson and Joseph Medill, founder of the *Chicago Tribune*. Potter Palmer opened a small dry goods store that eventually was to become the Marshall Field Store and make Field one of Chicago's greatest millionaires. Aaron Montgomery Ward was a travelling salesman for a St. Louis concern when he conceived the idea of selling by mail to the rural population. While the idea of the Pullman car was not George Pullman's, he built and operated sleeping cars in such quantities that his company became a monopoly and Pullman the generic name for the car. In 1881, Pullman began building his own feudal kingdom on the south side of Chicago. A model community for his workers, Pullman City was hailed as the start of a new era in the lives of working people. A little more than 10 years later, the workers who lived in the model city were bitter and disillusioned, a strike was declared and thousands of federal troops were sent to keep order in

Chicago. Pullman eventually won the victory, but Pullman City was never again the same.

It remained for the advent of the Civil War, with the corruption that always marches with war, to build the really great American fortunes. Jay Cooke and Jim Fiske formed an unholy alliance to battle Commodore Vanderbilt for control of the Erie Railroad. In the process, Boss Tweed ruled the Tammany ring in the New York City government, and thousands of small investors lost their money. Jay Gould, aided by Jim Fiske, manipulated President Grant in an attempt to corner the gold market. Before they were done, in the fall of 1869, half of Wall Street was in financial ruin.

And then the parade really began. Out of Pittsburgh came Andrew Carnegie and the Mellons; from Cleveland, John D. Rockefeller and the newly formed Standard Oil Company; in the West, the Four Horsemen of the Apocalypse—Charles Crocker, Leland Stanford, Mark Hopkins and Collis Potter Huntington—wrote a chapter in history comparable to that of Cooke, Fiske and Gould. Out of Philadelphia came the banking family of the Drexels, and from their stable came John Pierpont Morgan. From Illinois came John ''Bet-A-Million'' Gates and the American Steel and Wire Company; from Delaware came the DuPonts and their gun powder. With little apparent moral conscience, a public-be-damned attitude and meager government control, these men wheeled and dealed, purchased immunity and then received congratulations for being smart operators. That the fortunes were built upon the suffering and misery of the less fortunate was of little importance.

The industrialization of America had its beginning in the 1840s in the factories of New England, where women and children alike worked in the mills from sun up to sun down. There were no vacations, no fringe benefits, nothing but hard work and grinding poverty. If the workers attempted to form labor unions to better their lot, their efforts were quickly smashed. The Pinkerton National Detective Agency founded by Allen Pinkerton, a U.S. Secret Service agent during the Civil War, supplied spies and strikebreakers who used brute force to subdue the striking workers.

The Civil War had broken the back of agricultural slavery, which now was not needed as badly as a new slave force to serve the industrial revolution. And to serve in these ranks were the millions of immigrants who began to stream into the country in the 1870s. America was the end of the rainbow, the Garden of Eden and Heaven wrapped up in one package to the newcomers. Most of the immigrants thought they were escaping to a better way of life. Instead of finding the pot of gold,

Adelina Patti theater program, c. 1890s.

Women's Building at the Columbian Exposition, Chicago, 1893.

they found only the exchange of one kind of misery for another.

The panic of 1873, brought by the manipulations of Cooke, Fiske and Gould, caused millions of workers to lose their jobs as thousands of businesses failed. In New York during that winter, 900 persons starved to death, 3,000 infants were abandoned on doorsteps and more than 11,000 boys were left homeless. Men and women slept in hallways and public parks, unable to afford rent in even the worst of the miserable tenements.

The year of 1893 brought even worse conditions than the panic of 1873. Almost overnight, hundreds of thousands of workers found themselves jobless, with the number to rise eventually to more than four million. Ragged and hungry bands of jobless men began to haunt the city streets and swarm over the countryside, to find themselves treated as rabble. In Chicago, the relief centers and soup kitchens were hardly able to find enough food. And out along the lakefront, the Columbian Exposition opened its doors to show the entire world the great progress America was making!

For the extremely wealthy, the '90s were truly gay. Happily they splashed their wealth about, building bigger and bigger homes, entertaining lavishly. Since the greater number of jewels a wife could display, the greater the status of the husband, many women became walking diamond mines. Europe was looted of its paint-

ings, statuary and priceless antiquities to grace the brownstone monuments of ego; titled European nobility were purchased as husbands for the wealthy American daughters; thus was born the image of the "Ugly American."

The same intensity the Victorians displayed in stuffing their homes with European loot and horsehair sofas also was applied to their clothing. Personal adornment in both dress and jewelry reached dizzying heights. The more ribbons, beads, flounces and lace hung on the clothing, so much the better. It was a race between old wealth and new wealth. As soon as a fashion was adopted by the old rich, the *nouveau riche* began the process of imitation. While the previous two centuries had seen the rise of fashion, it remained for the Victorians to tie on all the tassels, which they did in great abundance.

Such was the warp and woof of Victorian life in America. The era saw the expansion of industry, the building of labor unions, the extremes of poverty and wealth, the change from a rural society to an urban society. Manners were stilted and strained, the literature dripped with sentiment and the poetry was even worse. Everything had to be proper and in good taste; there were rigid rules of dress, etiquette and conduct. God was in his highest, and the grim reaper often walked the land.

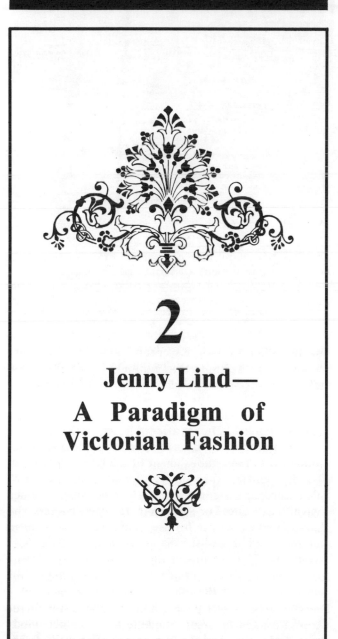

THE WAY IT WAS

2

Jenny Lind—
A Paradigm of Victorian Fashion

When Jenny began her American tour in 1850, the houses were packed in New York, Boston, Providence, Baltimore and Philadelphia; her southern tour included the cities of Washington, Richmond, Charleston, Havana (Cuba), New Orleans, Natchez, Memphis, St. Louis, Nashville, Louisville and Cincinnati. The Jenny Lind fever, or "Lindomania," swept the country. There were Jenny Lind beds, clothing, glassware, jewelry, buttons, shawls, capes, parasols, cigars (Jenny hated the smell of cigar smoke) and even Jenny Lind soup. Two special flowers were named after her. She met such greats as Henry Clay, Daniel Webster and Longfellow; the President and his family entertained her at the Capitol in Washington.

P.T. Barnum led the pack when he erected his home near Bridgeport, Connecticut. Having seen Prinny's Pavilion of Brighton, Barnum decided that was just the kind of home he needed. Named Iranistan, the house was a nightmare combination of Byzantine, Moorish and Turkish architecture, with its minarets and spires poking their way to the heavens. A conservatory formed a big bulge at either end of the building. The large and beautifully landscaped grounds were dotted with fountains and stocked with iron deer and elk in the current Victorian tradition. A large winding staircase led up from the main hall; the panels of the drawing room represented the four seasons and the ceiling was white and gold. A Chinese library with Chinese furniture adjoined the dining room. The walls of Barnum's private study were brocaded with rich orange satin. Jenny was properly impressed with Iranistan and her comment, translated into today's language, was: "Anyone who could build something like this can't be all bad" (Jenny never completely trusted Barnum). Unfortunately for posterity, a workman carelessly left a lighted pipe on a cushioned seat and Iranistan burned to the ground in 1857.

Of three major collections in the United States of Lind memorabilia, two now are in museums. The first was that of Leonidas Westervelt, who began collecting around 1900. His collection is at the New York Historical Society. The second collection was that of Wm. Hildebrand, whose Lind collection is now in the Museum of the City of New York. The third collection belongs to W. Porter Ware, of Tennessee, recently retired after 43 years of service at the University of the South.

9

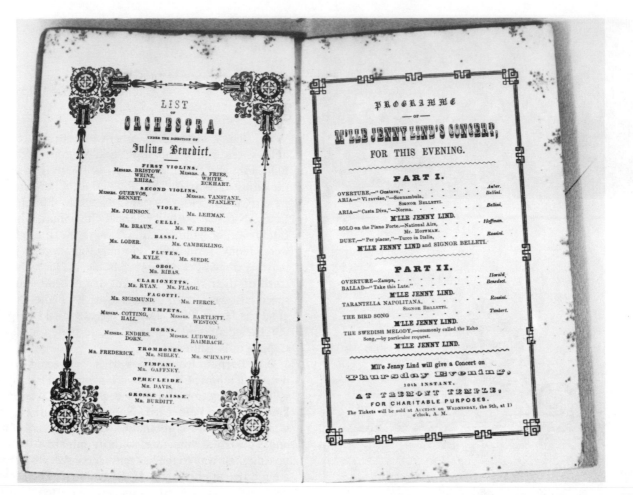

Interior of Jenny Lind concert program, Boston, 1850.

Mr. Ware is co-author of the book *The Lost Letters of Jenny Lind*, published in 1966; he is presently at work on his second Lind book, this one about her tour of America and Cuba between 1850 and 1852. The concert was given in Boston, with Julius Benedict, conductor; Giovanni Belletti, baritone, along with the ever present P.T. Barnum (see photo of theater program).

The cameo featured on the book jacket was sent to Mr. Ware to ascertain whether or not it might be a Jenny Lind cameo. Mr. Ware did not feel he could give a positive identification because of the difference in hair styling. Nathaniel Willis Parker, editor of the *Home Journal* in the 1850s once wrote that he had seen hundreds of "likenesses" of Jenny Lind in paintings, prints and drawings, but that he could not ever recall seeing one that really looked like her!

Great Victorian Women

From the San Francisco Call—June 21, 1903: "Berlin, June 20—Some time since the *Tageblatt* conducted a unique voting contest as to the ten greatest living men. A later question put to vote by the same paper was, who are the five greatest living women. The balloting has been completed and the results are as follows:

First of all came Baroness Bertha von Suttner, whose famous book, "Die Waffen Hieder" (Down With Arms), prompted the czar to issue his peace manifesto, which led to the establishment of the peace tribunal at The Hague. Her work in the interest of all manner of philanthropic enterprises is world renowned. Carmen Sylva, the ex-queen of Roumania, the sweet poetess who has labored all her life for the advancement of women, is next. Third in the list is Sarah Bernhardt, France's, if not the world's, greatest living actress. She is followed by Eleonore Duse, whom most of the Germans like much better than Bernhardt. It is strange that not a single native of Germany proved a favorite with the *Tageblatt* readers. Baroness von Ebner Eschenbach, who is last on the list, being an Austrian by birth, though her voluminous writings and poems are all in German."

THE WAY IT WAS

3

The Prophetic Charts

The prophetic charts illustrated in this chapter were used by the followers of Rev. Miller in preaching the belief of an imminent doomsday and the return of Christ. The camp meeting system has been credited to this group; John Greenleaf Whittier wrote an account of his attendance at one of these meetings:

American Progress: or The Great Events of the Greatest Century, by Hon. R.M. Devens of Massachusetts. Published by Hugh Heron, Chicago, Ill. 1886 Edition:

"On my way eastward, I spent an hour or two at a camp ground of the Second Advent in East Kingston, N.H. Set in a growth of pine and hemlock, several hundred, perhaps a thousand people were present and more were rapidly coming. Drawn about in a circle were the white tents and back of them the provision stalls and cook shops. Suspended from the front of the rude pulpit were two broad sheets of canvas, upon one of which was the figure of a man—the head of gold, the breast and arms of silver, the belly of brass, the legs of iron and the feet of clay—the dream of Nebuchadnezzar! On the other were depicted the wonders of the Apocalyptic vision—the beasts—the dragons—the scarlet woman seen by the seer of Patmos—oriental types and figures and mystic symbols translated into startling Yankee realities, and exhibited like the beasts of a travelling menagerie. One horrible image with its hideous heads and scaly caudal extremity, reminded me of the tremendous line of Milton, who, in speaking of the same evil dragon, described him 'as swinging the scaley horrors of his folded tail.' To an imaginative mind, the scene was full of novel interest. The white circle of tents—the dim wood arches—the upturned earnest faces—the loud voices of the speakers, burdened with the awful symbolic language of the Bible—the smoke from the fires rising like incense from forest altars—carried one back to the days of primitive worship, when 'the groves were God's first temples'."

One of the folklore legends that arose about the believers said that as the anticipated day arrived, they would don their ascension robes and mount to the rooftops awaiting the coming of the Lord. When the expected event did not materialize, the aftermath was termed the "Great Disappointment." Many of the followers, disenchanted, left the movement and returned to their original churches. Those that remained eventually broke off into two groups, one becoming the Seventh Day Adventist Church and the second the Advent Christian Church.

Unlike the stormy end of the life of Mormon Joseph Smith, Rev. Miller lived to the age of 68, at peace, still working within his church. As late as 1894, Joshua V. Himes, one of the early leaders of the movement, refuted the ascension robe legend: "The statement that 'to be prepared, dressed in their ascension robes, was the instruction given by their leaders to the rank and file of the Millerites' is almost too silly to be noticed."

Forty five miles southwest of Chicago lies the campus of Aurora College, founded in 1893 by Advent Christian Church. On the second floor of its library is a room bearing the name "Jenks Collection." Contained in this room are hundreds of books, magazines and letters dealing with the early history of the Millerite movement. Stern, but twinkling-eyed, Dr. Orrin Roe Jenks was an early president of the college, possessed with a keen sense of history. Throughout his lifetime, Dr. Jenks patiently gathered together much of this material, including the charts that have been photographed expressly for this book. To this quiet room have come scholars and theologians from all corners of the world to study and research this marvelously complete collection; from these studies many doctoral dissertations have been written.

The Rev. Wm. Miller (The Prophet).
(Aurora College, see Credits.)

The Prophetic Charts (right), top to bottom: Painted on cloth; lithograph published by Joshua Himes; hand-painted on canvas. (Aurora College, see Credits.)

FASHION DOLLS AND FASHION PLATES

4

The Fashion Babies

Fashion, as we perceive it today, had its earliest beginnings in the luxurious courts of France and Burgundy, when cultural life began to center in the towns. Essentially, fashion was the sole province of the nobility, and was to remain so until the 17th Century.

Jeanne de Bourbon, wife of Charles V of France (1364-1380) is distinguished in history as the first fashion leader. Hers was the world of the handsome velvets, silks and brocades of Italy. But France was beginning to take its first step toward domination of the world of fashion; the art of weaving and dyeing made so much progress that people of all classes were clothed in material of excellent quality.

Isabella of Bavaria, wife of Charles VI (1380-1422), was the first to gain a European reputation for inaugurating changes in fashion. She also was the first to make use of fashion dolls, or fashion babies as they became known, when she sent several to the Queen of England (wife of Henry IV, 1367-1413) to show the court fashions. Separated by the Channel, what better way for two queens to promote friendly relations, gossiping over the back fence about a shared interest? If, in the process, trade and commerce were improved by the visit of the dolls, so much the better. The dolls that Isabella sent on their long journey were the first of a long line of dolls eventually sent to other parts of Europe, and finally to the New World.

Isabella, Queen of Spain and patroness to Christopher Columbus, received a life-sized fashion doll as a gift from Anne of Brittany, Queen of France, in 1496.

After his divorce from his first wife in 1601, Henry IV of France, anxious to please, wrote to his betrothed, Maria de Medicis: "Frontenc tells me that you desire patterns of our fashion in dress. I send you therefore some model dolls."

Jean Baptiste Colbert (1619-83), Minister of France under Louis XIV, once served as an apprentice in a woolen draper's shop, and was more than cognizant of the value of export trade in fabrics. As a result of his able administration, the first lace factories came into being in France and everything possible was done to encourage the use of French needlepoints. When Louis XIV (1643-1715) finally established himself as absolute monarch in 1661, court clothing became laden with lace, ribbons and ruffles. Paris became the center of fashion and good taste, a position she held for the next 250 years.

The most famous of the fashion dolls originated in the Hotel de Rambouillet of Paris. The house previously was called the Hotel Pisini, the residence of the Marquis of that name. His daughter, Catherine de Vivonne, received it as a part of her dowry on her marriage in 1600 with the future Marquis de Rambouillet. Not content with the style of the house, she had it entirely remodelled between 1610 and 1617. After its completion, Catherine, weary of the crowded assemblies of the Louvre, decided to remain at the house and make her home the center of her social activities. The brilliant intellectuals of France—known, from their insistence on refined speech and manners, as précieux—assembled here for a generation.

Among the early frequenters were Richelieu, Malherbe, Balzac, Corneille, Racine,Voltaire. Here, too, the young ladies were trained who were destined to found literary salons in their turn—Madame de la Fayette, Madeleine de Scudery, The Duchess of Longueville and Madame de Sevigne. Under the leadership of Madeleine de Scudery (1607-1701), later a prolific novelist, the young ladies dressed the dolls and exhibited them with each change of style. One, called "La Grande Pandore," was shown in full dress; the other, "La Petite Pandore," was in the "politest undress." Replicas of the dolls were then sent to costume designers in London, Madrid, Vienna, Rome and Berlin, with Jean Colbert making certain the dolls reached their destination.

The fashion-minded women of the other countries could either copy the style of fashion from the dolls or adapt them to their own taste. The dolls must have caused a sensation, for as early as 1645, German women were being satirized by their nation's writers for sending to France for the dolls.

Hotel Rambouillet began to decline after the marriage (in 1645) of the daughter of the house to the Duc de Montausier; the death of M. de Rambouillet in 1652 and Catherine's increasing age and ill health finally brought the reign of the house to a close.

But the fashion dolls retained their popularity. They had made their mark in the world. England was becoming more and more fashion conscious: London received the dolls four times a year—spring, summer, autumn and winter—and adapted them to English taste. The fashion babies were called "The Dolls of the Rue St. Honore" and "Les Grandes courriers des Modes," and the English also began to make and export fashion dolls. The *Gentlemen's Magazine* for September, 1731, reported: "Several dolls with different dresses made in St. James Street have been sent to the Czarina to show the manner of dressing at present in fashion among English ladies."

Although the trip was a long one, the fashion dolls found their way to the colonies of the New World. Mrs. Vanderbilt, in her *Social History of Flatbush* commented: "We have a vivid remembrance of the old age of one of the fashion dolls which had been sent from Paris (1720) to a fashionable mantua maker in New York. When the dress was changed as to style, the dressmaker sold the doll to one of her customers, and "Miss Nancy Dawson" passed into the obscurity of humbler dollies, who had never been sent as ministers plenipotentiary from the Court of Fashion."

The New England Weekly Journal of July 2, 1733, carried the following advertisement: "To be seen at Mrs. Hannah Teatt's, Mantua Maker at the head of Summer Street, Boston, a baby drest after the newest fashion of Mantuas and Nightgowns and everything belonging to a dress. Latilly arrived on Captain White from London. Any Ladies that desire to see it may either come or send, she will be ready to wait on 'em; if they come to the House it is Two Shilling & if she waits on 'em, it is Seven Shilling."

One of the most colorful figures to emerge at this point in fashion history was Rose Bertin (1714-1813). Born in Amiens, Rose was told by a gypsy fortune teller that she would rise to fame and fortune. An ambitious woman, at the first opportunity she left for Paris where she was apprenticed to the small but fashionable millinery shop, "Trait Galan," of Mlle. Pagelle. It did not take long for Rose's charm and talent to attract women of royalty. In 1787, she was appointed Secretary of Fashion and dressmaker to Marie Antoinette.

Rose made life-sized fashion dolls, and miniature dolls showing the queen's fashions. These dolls, which were sold and displayed throughout Europe, served as models for the dressmakers.

Rose, fortunate in escaping the tragic end that was Marie Antoinette's, took her tirewomen and sempstresses to London. There she continued with her trade and French fashion found a home in England—but in turn, French fashion showed an English influence. Rose Bertin rose to fame and fortune as the gypsy foretold, but she also ended up in bankruptcy with debts totalling two million francs.

In 1764, a doll the size of a fully grown human being was sent to England from France, landing at Dover dressed in the finest lace. Even though the ports were closed during war time, the "Grand Courrier de la Mode" was always given safe passage—if she did not arrive safely, the war ministry heard from the ladies in no uncertain terms! The following from *The Spectator* is proof of the anxiety caused in London by an overdue fashion doll: "I was almost in despair of ever seeing a model from the dear country, when last Sunday I overhead a lady in the next pew to me whisper to another that at the Seven Stars in King Street, Covent Garden, there was a mademoiselle completely dressed just come from Paris. I was in the utmost impatience during the remaining part of the service, and as soon as ever it was over, having learnt the milliner's address, I went directly to her house in King Street, but was told the French lady was at a person of quality in Pall Mall and would not be back again until late that nite. I was therefore obliged to renew my visit this morning, and had then a full view of the dear puppet from head to foot. You cannot imagine how ridiculously I find that we have all been trussed up during the war and how infinitely the French dress excels ours.''

The fashion dolls were just as eagerly awaited in the New Republic. American women setting out for England were often implored to send back fashion babies. As soon as one arrived, it was the kind of news that had to be shared. Sally McKean wrote to the sister of Dolly Madison in June, 1796: "I sent yesterday to see a doll which has come from England, dressed to show the fashions.'' The war was over and English fashions were acceptable again.

The reign of the fashion doll began to crumble. She had been unchallenged for nearly 400 years, her subjects following every change of her dress. Looming on the horizon were the fashion periodicals and the fashion plates that were so much a part of the Victorian age. Retired with honor, the lovely little queens found their way from the milliners' boxes and mantua makers' show rooms to the nurseries and playrooms. Here they lived out their remaining years as beloved companions to the little people, who loved and cared for them.

"Miss Nancy Dawson"

Not all the fashion dolls went the way of most childhood toys. By a most fortunate stroke of luck, "Miss Nancy Dawson" has been located. The following letter was received from the Independence National Historical Park, 311-313 Walnut Street, Philadelphia, Pennsylvania:

"The wax fashion doll referred to as 'Miss Nancy Dawson' in Elizabeth McClellan's *History of American Costume* is indeed a part of the Collection of Independence National Historical Park. Our records show the doll was given to Sarah Duffield of Philadelphia by Mrs. John Penn in 1766. It has been in the Independence Hall Collection since 1874, the gift of Mrs. Bernard Henry. It is thus described on our catalogue card:

The doll is nine inches high; it is dressed in a Watteau sacque of taffeta (a white ground with crossbar lines of red) over a hooped petticoat trimmed with pink

Florence. The stomacher is plain without a point, finished with robings of silk from the shoulder to a little below the waist line. An apron of soft green silk is worn under the stomacher. The sleeves end at the elbow and are finished with graduated ruffles of silk, pinked very deep in the back and short in the front; a knot of red, the prevailing color of the costume, is on each sleeve and also in the hair, which was originally powdered and worn close to the head—probably in French curls. High-heeled slippers, a necklace and a bracelet complete the costume.''—Laurie Gearhart (Mrs. John Gearhart, III) museum technician.

Miss Nancy Dawson. (City of Philadelphia, see Credits.)

FASHION DOLLS AND FASHION PLATES

5

Fashion Plates— The Art

Toward the end of the fashion doll era, a new vehicle for fashion news emerged. Two noted engravers were directing their talents to fashion. Wenzel Hollar (1607-1676), in 1640, produced a collection of 26 pictures of Englishwomen with the title: *Ornatus Muliebris Anglicanus. The several Habits of Englishwomen, from the Nobilitie to the Country Women As they are in these Times.* Abraham Bosse (1602-1676), an engraver and etcher from Tours, France, produced some fashion engravings, probably executed from his own designs.

The first fashion periodical, without fashion plates, seems to have been the *Mercure galant*, later the *Mercure de France*, published in Paris in 1670. About 1690, Jean de Dieu (called Saint-Jean) and the Bonnart family made engravings that could have been used as fashion plates. These usually showed a single figure and bore such titles as "Lady of Quality in Winter Dress" and "Lady in Summer Dishabille" and were based on clothes worn in the French Court. Eventually these drawings found their way to other parts of Europe, as did the fashion dolls, but the use of the drawings diminished in the early part of the 18th century. Evidently, the fashion dolls still held the throne.

In 1778, two Parisian booksellers, Jacques Esnouts and Michel Rapilly, conceived the idea of issuing colored plates of the male and female fashions of the day. Their *Galerie des Modes et des Costumes Francais Dessinet D'apres Nature* was published until 1787, with illustrations by Claude Louis Desrois, Pierre Thomas LeClere, Francois Watteau de Lille and Augustin de Saint Aubin.

Italy, developing its own fashion centers during the same period—and not to be outdone by the French—began publishing its own fashion periodicals.

A French publication solely devoted to fashion was *Le Cabinet des Modes*, launched in 1785, with plates colored by hand. In the next 12 years the name of the magazine was changed several times; in 1797 it acquired its final name: *Le Journal des Dames et des Modes*. The magazine continued publication until 1839 under the leadership of an ecclesiastic named La Mesangere, who had been a professor of philosophy in the college of La Fleche. The good professor became so devoted to the love of dress that, at his death, his wardrobe held 2,000 pairs of shoes, 75 coats, 100 round hats and uncounted breeches. Every fifth day of his 30 years of reign, the Journal issued a colored plate of a fashionably dressed dame; on the fifteenth of each month, two larger and more important plates were issued.

It was not until 1770 in England that the systematic and widespread production of fashion prints began with *The Lady's Magazine*. Between 1771 and the early 1800s, several ladies' almanacks and annuals were born—into which one page of the latest hats or dresses was inserted. One of the first English prints, ready-tinted, was published in *The Lady's Magazine* in 1771. *The Gallery of Fashion*, probably the most luxuriant of all fashion periodicals, was created in England by a German artist, Nicolaus von Heideloff. It was quarto size instead of the smaller octavo and its subscribers were from the exclusive society and royalty. Unfortunately, it had a short life, disappearing from the fashion scene in 1803.

Another of the early English fashion magazines was *The Ladies European Magazine*, edited by a group of women and first published in London in 1798. Another, *La Belle Assemblies*, or *Bell's Court and Fashionable Magazine*, was issued regularly in London from 1806 to 1832, when a new series was started. The Hon. Mrs. Norton was editor, and its name was changed to *The Court Magazine and Monthly Critic*. This periodical was as popular in the United States as it was in England. A letter from Paris every month kept its readers in touch with the court of the "Great Mogul," the name Walpole gave to fashion. The *Calendar of the English Court*, which formed the supplement of the second series, evidently was read with great interest on both sides of the ocean.

Ackermann's *Repository of Arts, Literature, Commerce, Manufactures, Fashions and Politics*, published in London in 1809, was another popular periodical that contained fashion plates of the latest modes. In Philadelphia, *Mr. Dennie's Port Folio* appeared with the first year of the century and continued until 1805 and gave a column or more of its racy pages to the novelties of the season. Under the heading "Festoon of Fashion," a brief review of the modes in France and England was given; "Mr. Oldschool" (pen name of the editor) used pen portraits of the costumes.

Paris retained its position as the home of high fashion for the ladies, however, and it wasn't long before French fashion plates appeared in the magazines of other countries. There was no copyright law (nor would there be in America until the end of the 19th Century), and it was a simple matter to steal and reprint fashion plates. They usually were a year or more old when they were re-engraved and reprinted, but that was of little importance since fashions did not change as rapidly as they do today. The first French prints began to appear in the English *Lady's Magazine* in 1785; in time, both the English and the French prints were pirated.

The periodical most associated with fashion plates in America is *Godey's Lady's Book*, which began publication in Philadelphia in 1830. Godey claimed his was the oldest magazine in America, a statement he ran on the back cover of his periodical time and again. In truth, the first magazine to be printed was the Philadelphia-based *American Magazine*, published by Andrew Bradford. It appeared February 13, 1741, and preceded by three days the publication date of Franklin's *General Magazine*. The *Casket,* also based in Philadelphia, had its beginning in 1826, and Sarah Hale of Boston started a small woman's magazine in 1828. *Godey's*, the *Casket* and Sarah's magazine each issued unacknowledged re-engravings of Paris originals, and followed the general format established by *The Court*. Serial stories, poetry and editorial comments filled the little octavos. The pirated fashion plates, or "embellishments" as Godey called them, were the extra goodie thrown in to please the ladies despite the opposition of some influential citizens.

The success and long life of the *Godey's Lady's Book* came from the unique combination of Louis Godey and Sarah Josepha Hale. Godey began publishing on a shoe string; for the first six and a half years he was publisher, editor, chief cook and bottle washer. For all his brashness and loudness, Godey was first of all a good businessman; he knew he needed a good editor, and for this he chose Sarah Hale. Persuading Sarah to join his ranks was not easy, but his persistence finally won her over, and Sarah's magazine was merged with Godey's in 1836. She became editor and held the post for the next 40 years.

Sarah Hale's first stroke of luck was her family's belief that education should be extended to the girls as well as to the boys; her second in that her husband did not agree with the adage that women should be beautiful but dumb. Before his early death, the couple would read and discuss history, law and literature. This training served her well when she suddenly was left with five children to support and little money. A soft, gentle, compassionate woman, Sarah was gifted with vision for the future. The quiet voice that strengthened Lord Russell's campaign for Queen Victoria was equally adept in speaking for the needs of women. Sarah was a pen-in-hand general, using the art of gentle persuasion to convince men that a better lot for women would yield the benefits of happier wives and daughters. Sarah was indeed the perfect foil to the brash W.C. Field character of Louis Godey. Always the polite gentleman, Godey addressed his subscribers as his "dear ladies," while Sarah spoke calmly and forcefully for goodness and virtue (more on Sarah Hale's life in Chapter 11). Together, they were the living, breathing models for the Victorian view of the perfect lady and gentleman. To-

Columbian Magazine, 1846.

gether, they made the *Godey's Lady's Book* a household word to American women.

Godey's first issue contained a water-colored fashion plate of French origin. At first, there were hand-colored plates every three months; soon this was increased to one in each issue. The plates remained a single sheet for the first 30 years. After 1861, double plates were published that had to be folded to fit the octavo size of the magazine. The early plates usually contained one or two figures; the double plates often contained as many as five or six figures showing the latest styles and were water-colored by hand. Godey never failed to mention to his "dear ladies": "Let it be remembered that Godey originated the double fashion plate, as he has originated everything that is valuable in magazine embellishment;" and "Godey's Fashions are the only correct ones given in the United States. Others give colored figures, not caring whether they are fashion or not." A truly modest fellow!

To compete with *Godey's*, the *Casket* began to publish fashion plates in 1831; their first plate showed Queen Adelaide in a very fancy dress. These appeared at the rate of one or two a year until 1836, when there were four. George R. Graham took over publication of the magazine in 1840. One of his first decisions was to change the policy common to the monthly magazines—that of publishing impressions from used steel and copper plates. Nothing but the best for Graham—only new plates were to be used, engraved expressly for *Graham's*.

Other periodicals were springing to life, their format the same as *Godey's*. *Snowden's Ladies' Companion* was born in 1834, lasting just 10 years—until 1844. *Miss Leslie's Magazine* appeared in 1843, published until 1846, when it merged with *Godey's*. The *Columbian Magazine* was launched in New York by Israel Post in 1844 but it, too, had a short life, disappearing in 1849. Sarah and Godey were a tough combination to beat. *Peterson's Ladies' National Magazine* started in 1842; *Arthur's Home Gazette*, started in 1850, changed its name to *Arthur's Home Magazine* in 1853. These two had staying power, and with *Godey's*, remained running mates for the remainder of the century. Together they shared the final hour of defeat when all ceased publication in 1898.

Frank Leslie's Ladies Gazette of Fashion came into being in 1854, changed the name to *Frank Leslie's Lady's Magazine* in 1857, continuing publication until 1882. With the exception of *Leslie's*, most of the periodicals were of the octavo size, their contents and style so alike it would have been possible to swap covers, with no one the wiser. And all contained the fashion plates so eagerly studied by fashion-conscious American women.

Peterson's Magazine, 1864.

Harper's Monthly Magazine, 1855; signature,
Voigt, del Roberts, Sc.

Demorest plate from Ladies' Own Magazine, 1873.

One of the comic side-plays during this era was the sniping Godey and Graham aimed at each other. When Godey prattled on about the virtues of *his* magazine, Graham replied in like vein (December 1852): "It is not our purpose to show off, to take airs, to be proud... but our new type, our new coat which covers it, and the very superior quality of our whole rig is rather stared at, we know. Excessive modesty has been our weakness—it is the besetting frailty of most Magazine publishers, as is fully evinced in their prospectuses. Why should Graham be proud? That question rather startles us; but the answer is at hand—because he has the greatest Magazine in the world—and the prettiest girls, and the most of 'em—to read it. It is estimated that 60,000 beautiful women are in love with *Graham*—the Magazine, of course—and Graham is as proud as Lucifer about it." Another modest fellow!

The first magazine to break the mold appeared in 1860—*Madame Demorest's Mirror of Fashions*. Ellen and Kate Curtis, later the founders of the publication, became fashion-oriented as they grew up in the Saratoga Springs resort area. Ellen trained as a milliner and dressmaker, her path eventually leading to New York and marriage to William Jennings Demorest. In her sister Kate and her husband William, Ellen found two staunch allies who helped lay the foundation of her idea of paper patterns for home sewers. William was a natural promotor, with a liberal dash of P.T. Barnum and Louis Godey; he also was a tinkerer and inventor. One of his early inventions was a small portable bake oven. Displaying it at the offices of the *Scientific American Magazine*, William baked a batch of bread to prove how well his invention worked.

Ellen and Kate had developed model dress charts for children that won two prize medals for them at the Crystal Palace in New York in 1853. Ellen's plan to create dress patterns from tissue paper followed. By 1859, Madame Demorest's establishment was a growing concern at 375 Broadway, three doors above Taylor's Saloon. Her patterns were described as "the result of great taste and skill, combined with frequent intercourse with the best foreign houses; and are so various that every style of person may be suited from her emporium."

Ebenezer Butterick generally has been credited with the innovation of paper dress patterns—only because he patented the idea in 1863. His patterns evolved from long experience in making clothing for boys and men. For all his smarts, this was the one time that William Jennings Demorest missed the boat.

Demorest Magazine, 1886.

When the *Mirror* was first published, the patterns were advertised and a sample attached as a premium, with instructions on how to use it. Women studied the fashion plates, tried the sample patterns and clamored for more. In 1864, the magazine was reorganized under the name *Demorest's Illustrated Monthly Magazine and Mme. Demorest's Mirror of Fashions*.

Ellen and Kate modified the frivolous French fashions to present American women with styles that were practical, yet elegant. The fashions were created from original European models, and the plates in the magazine were based on actual clothing, not on reproductions of old French plates. Madame Demorest also cre-

ated what must have been the fashion plate to end all fashion plates—a full yard wide and three-quarters of a yard high, with more than 70 gowns illustrated. It was printed on heavy plate paper, elegantly colored, varnished and mounted on a roller. For just $1.00 you could purchase the plate, postage paid, and receive with it a booklet entitled "What to Wear."

Ladies Own Magazine originated in 1869 in Indianapolis, moved to Chicago after the great fire, and was published by M. Cora Bland Co. The 1873 volume contains a mixture of French and what appear to be American plates. Of particular interest is the magazine's June, 1873, announcement, which stated: "We have

REVIEW OF FASHIONS.—JANUARY.

FASHION has laid aside all tendencies to conservatism and exclusiveness in the choice of fabrics, and all materials are admissible, provided that the artistic and graceful enter into their making up. Of course there are individual preferences, but these are not permitted to affect the general tone of prevailing styles.

Woolen materials for costumes are especially popular at present, but not to the exclusion of other goods to a degree that one needs to feel unfashionable if arrayed in a suit of silk, satin or velvet. Indeed the amount of good black silk sold and worn is almost incredible. This is not, however, so much the case in New York City as in almost any other portion of the country. Here there are continual arrivals of wool novelties to distract the attention from standard fabrics, and as the central point in the most fashionable dry goods houses is the wool goods counter, it is not strange that ladies select from these most attractive materials.

The New York woman revels in wool novelties at present, and it would seem that the more they resemble an army blanket the more she dotes on them. Indeed the popular devotion of the fashionable fair ones is divided between this class of goods and the *frisé* and *bouclé* novelties, which are, in some grades and weights, fast reaching a pitch of absurdity. If a woman were compelled to carry about her the same number of pounds that are represented by the amount of cloth of the *frisé* or plush order necessary to make a fashionable walking costume, she would be astonished to have such an unreasonable demand made upon her. It is no easy task for an ordinarily muscular salesman to handle a full piece of these goods, and as there are rarely more than three dresses in a piece, and still more weight in the way of linings, trimming and the combination material, which is usually heavier still, it may be readily understood that to be fashionable in the selection of dress goods is to impose upon one's self a burden not only grievous in point of weariness, but dangerous to the health. When to the dress is added the weight of the outside garment and other clothing, the only wonder is that a woman can walk at all.

It is a perfectly safe prediction that the reign of these immensely heavy suitings will be short. They have no great durability, and while they are undeniably stylish, they will wear out the bodies and tempers of even ordinarily strong women. They might be used to advantage for carriage dresses, and to this use the heavier and more elegant materials will undoubtedly come.

The newest arrivals in wool goods are wool plushes in stripes nearly two inches wide, alternating with the same width stripe in a very pronounced diagonal. The stripes run lengthwise of the goods, and the colors are the various shades of brown, gray, olive and a shade of navy blue. Plain goods like the diagonal stripe are provided to match. The most approved style for making these is to use the plain goods for a short postilion basque and sleeves, and for the full, straight back draperies. Three breadths of the plush striped goods are required for the front and side breadths,

(*Continued on page* 196.)

COUPON ORDER

Good for one Paper Pattern before February 15th, 1886.

Run name or pencil through the name and size of pattern desired.

☞ **Example :** 1. Colandine Wrapper, 34, 36, 38, 40 Bust Measure.

1. Lafontaine Toilet. 34, 36, 38 and 40 Bust Measure.
2. Hermione Costume. 34, 36, 38 and 40 Bust Measure.
3. Beatrice Jacket. 34, 36, 38 and 40 Bust Measure.
4. Medora Visite. Medium and Large Sizes.
5. Procida Skirt. Medium Size.
6. Gentleman's Morning Jacket. Medium and Large Sizes.
7. Elisa Costume. 8, 10 and 12 Years.
8. Ulina Coat. 4, 6, 8 and 10 Years.
9. Infant's Sacque Cloak. 6 months to 1 year, and 2 Years.
10. Lilla Hood. 6 to 8, 10 to 12, and 14 to 16 Years.
11. Wilhelm Suit. 6, 8 and 10 Years.
12. Tam O'Shanter Cap. 4, 6 and 8 Years.

Name,

Street and Number

Post-Office,

County, State,

.... 1886.

W. JENNINGS DEMOREST,
17 East 14th Street, New York.

Inclosed find a two cent postage stamp with Coupon Order for the cut paper pattern **Marked Out** *from list above, and illustrated in the number for January, 1886.*

Demorest Magazine, 1886—opening page of fashion section of magazine.

Godey's Lady's Book, 1892; signature, PM.

closed a contract with Madame Demorest, by which we are able to give the fashion plates and complete descriptions of styles from advanced sheets of her fashion monthly, so that they will appear in the two magazines, *Demorests* and *Ladies Own* simultaneously . . . Madame Demorest avails herself of the leading and important fashion designs in Europe and America. She prunes off an absurdity here, and adds a touch of elegance there, as one having authority, until Demorest's fashions stand unequalled in point of elegance, simplicity and fitness.''

At the close of its Volume VII, 1873, *Ladies Own* proudly announced that the editorial management of the fashion department by Madame Demorest had been so successful that the contract was renewed for 1874. Whatever the reason, *Ladies Own* ceased publication in 1874.

Harper's Monthly Magazine, beginning with Vol. I, 1850, through Vol. 30, 1864, presented a single page of fashion each month, printed on both sides. These were in black and white, similar to the regular utilitarian engravings contained in *Godey's*. It was no accident that *Harper's Monthly* discontinued its fashion page in

1864—*Harper's Bazar* was being readied for publication and started in 1867.

According to its first editorial, the *Bazar's* aim was to be a publication that would combine the useful and the beautiful. Special arrangements had been made with leading European journals, particularly with the German *Der Bazar*, whereby *Harper's* would receive fashion designs in advance and publish them at the same time they appeared in Paris, Berlin and other European cities. Fashions in vogue in New York—the Paris of America—also would be featured.

The first issue consisted of 16 pages in small folio, containing patterns, many large woodcuts of styles, serial fiction and miscellany. The fashion plates came directly from Berlin in the shape of duplicate electrotypes made by *Der Bazar*. With the plates came advance proofs of the letterpress describing the continental modes. The *Bazar* was a weekly magazine, a practice it continued until 1901, when it became a monthly magazine. In time, its size became more than double the usual octavo size. *Harper's* was different from the other fashion periodicals in that it was aimed at the wealthy woman.

The Delineator, 1896.

Thus ran the separate rivers of fashion in America. *Godey's, Peterson's* and *Arthur's* devoted many of their pages to the black and white woodcut engravings of the practical, everyday wear; as Godey put it, "Our wood engravings of the very latest fashions will be found useful for those who make their own dresses, and for those who make dresses for others." The pirated French or English plates simply were added as an embellishment to keep up circulation. Madame Demorest combined the best of European fashion with her own talents and those of the capable staff she later assembled. Her fashions were suited to the emerging, wealthier middle class. *Harper's Bazar* appealed to the extremely wealthy, promoting the era of haute couture emerging in Paris.

In 1864, Ebenezer Butterick moved to New York from Massachusetts and began publication of his first fashion plates, designed to promote his patterns. His first publications, the *Ladies' Quarterly Report of Broadway Fashions* and the *Metropolitan*, eventually evolved into the *Delineator,* which first appeared in 1872. Instead of cut steel plates, woodcuts were used for illustrations. The magazine also gave patterns as premiums, just as Madame Demorest had done 12 years earlier. The *Delineator* was followed by the *Woman's Home Companion* in 1873, the *Ladie's Home Journal* in 1883, and *Good Housekeeping* in 1885.

Peterson's had followed the Godey formula in its use of hand-colored fashion plates. Beginning in 1878, and continuing for 15 years thereafter, a paper pattern was issued with the magazine. *Arthur's* added hand-colored fashion plates about 1854. By 1880, free Butterick dress patterns became a part of the magazine, which were reproduced in four pages of its advertising section. In 1888, it adopted McCall patterns and stapled into the magazine James McCall & Company's monthly pattern and fashion periodical called the *Queen* (started in 1872), the forerunner of *McCall's Magazine.*

The Leslie publications used Parisian fashion plates, but occasionally other plates were credited to London or New York. The plates were on a par with those of *Godey's,* but larger, since the magazines were of a larger size. In June, 1862, one plate was published showing 29 figures, although it was a wood cut, not steel. In 1864, the magazine experimented with hand-colored lithographs—it had published three in 1857—using them for a year or two, often in a double page. By 1870, the magazines returned to the old-fashioned, hand-colored steel plates, sometimes using three in an issue, but without the foldover that Godey used.

By the 1880s, wood engraving had nearly replaced steel engraving as the medium for fashion plates. Lithography was used more and more in the fashion magazines, although the best magazines continued to have hand-colored plates until about the turn of the century.

The early French plates truly were fashion plates, since they were based not on actual articles of dress; but rather, they intended to whet the fashion appetite. The early fashion drawings by Voigt and later those of Madame Demorest were trade plates, as were the later French plates that listed the shops in which the articles of clothing could be purchased.

Madame Demorest's magazine followed *Godey's, Peterson's* and *Arthur's* into oblivion in 1899. Their passing marked the end of a very special era in the fashion life of America. By the turn of the century, the beautiful fashion plates so loved by American women slowly faded from sight. Whether they were true fashion plates, trade plates, steel, wood, original, stolen, good, bad or indifferent made little difference to the women in sod huts on a Kansas plain, those travelling by covered wagon with the precious periodical tucked safely in a corner of the wagon, or struggling with the crops on a remote farm in northern Wisconsin. The fashion plates were the stuff that dreams were made of and helped to brighten the lives of the Victorian women.

Lady's Book Fashions for November, 1836; signature,
Eldredge, Sc.

Godey's Americanized Paris Fashions, 1848;
signature, Heloise.

AN EQUESTRIAN FASHION PLATE.

Dedicated to the Lady readers of Godey

*An Equestrian Fashion Plate, 1849, dedicated to the lady
readers of Godey; signature, J.B. Neagle Sc.*

*Godey's Paris Fashions Americanized, 1849, engraved express-
ly for Godey's Lady's Book by J.I. Pease.*

*Graham's Paris Fashions, 1852; signature, Jules David (artist)
—Reville, engraver.*

LES MODES PARISIENNES.
AUGUST.
1864.

Les Modes Parisiennes, August, 1864, Peterson's Magazine;
engraved and printed by Illman Brothers.

*Front cover of The Delineator, August, 1906—The Gibson
Girl look. (Artist: Guernsey Moore)*

LES MODES PARISIENNES: PETERSON'S MAGAZINE.
MARCH, 1887. THE LETTER.

FASHION DOLLS AND FASHION PLATES

6

The Artists

One of the fascinating aspects of fashion plate study, as well as the most frustrating, is the attempt to discover the name of the original fashion artist and/or engraver. The early American plates—1830 to 1840—rarely were identified by signatures, although now and then one might pop up. One Godey plate of 1836 has the name of Eldredge Sc noted; an 1848 plate has the signature of Heloise; two 1849 plates bear the signatures of J.I. Pease and J.B. Neagle, Sc. Another researcher has added the names of A.W. Graham, F. Humphreys and A.H. Ritchie to the list of engravers producing plates for Godey.

The Godey plates were hand-colored in the beginning, and Godey spoke with pride of "our corps of one hundred and fifty female colorers." Unfortunately, the hand colorists of whom Godey was so proud often switched from one color to another if the first color ran out. Should the "dear ladies" complain of this, Godey had a ready answer. "We now colour our plates to different patterns so that two persons in a place may compare their fashions and adopt those colours that they suppose may be most suitable to their figures and complexions."

The *Broadway Journal* remarked in 1845: "Godey keeps almost as many ladies in his pay as the Grand Turk," and when there is an "interested clamour raised in certain quarters against the publication of fashion plates" he indignantly asserts that his plates are "a good service to the cause of civilization." While Mr. Godey lived, the hand-colored plates were never abandoned for long, though lithographs and other methods of color reproduction were attempted from time to time.

In 1840, when George Graham announced the change to the use of new plates only, he also hired John Sartain to work exclusively as an engraver for the magazine. By 1852, this arrangement evidently had changed, for Graham announced: "Our Paris Fashions cost us $945.00 per month for designing, engraving, printing and coloring." By importing the completed plates, Graham added the work of some of the best fashion artists of Europe to the American periodical, notably Anais Toudouze and Jules David.

The *Columbian Magazine* of the 1840s began to use the plates of *Les Modes Parisiennes, La Sylphide* and *Le Follet*, with the notation on the bottom of the plate, "Engraved Expressly for Columbian Magazine." They probably were the used or second-hand plates that Graham had refused to use. Again, this brought European fashion artists into an American periodical, and some of these plates also have been attributed to Anais Toudouze.

Columbian Magazine, 1845.

Leslie's, 1862.

Leslie's, 1859.

Beginning in the 1850s, publication of periodicals literally exploded at the seams. To keep up with the demand for fashion plates, the Yankee know-how of Currier and Ives probably was adopted. The Currier and Ives prints were produced first in black and white, then hand-colored on a production-line basis by a crew of colorists, each of whom applied one color. At times, some of the coloring was done by craftsmen not connected with the firm—a form of subcontract work.

P.K. Kimmel, an engraver of vignettes and portraits, was working in New York about 1850. The firm of Capewell and Kimmel was formed, which later became Kimmel and Foster. C. Foster was a designer and bank note engraver in the 1850s in Cincinnati, Ohio; he evidently joined the firm sometime in the 1860s. The 1857, 1858 and 1862 fashion plates in the Leslie publications carried the signature of the Capewell and Kimmel firm, as did 1864 plates in *Godey's.*

TEA GOWN FROM WORTH *(12.12.1891, p. 957).* This gown is a masterpiece, unique in design and in materials. It is a long flowing caftan of beige-colored cloth, draped over a velvet gown which fits the slender figure with sheath-like closeness. *Velours frappé* (stamped velvet) with maroon design on lighter ground, is used for the front of the close gown; it is fitted by darts and extends far back on the sides, fastening invisibly on the left. The fronts frame the slight figure with wide revers of white plush; their fulness is narrowly massed on the shoulders, with ends carried thence to the middle of the back, and knotted there above full back breadths that fall in Watteau-like pleats. A high collar has velvet at the back, and is covered in front with white lace extending lower in a pointed plastron. Deep cuffs of lace are on the sleeves.

Harper's Bazar 1891; signature, A. Sandoz.

*Godey's Lady's Book, 1864;
signature, L.T. Voigt, artist.*

a   *b*   *c*   *d*

DIFFERENT SKATING COSTUMES (*2.6.1869, cover*). **Fig. a:** dress of dark gray corduroy with fur trimming. The upper skirt is looped on the side and trimmed with a bow. The paletot is of black velvet with a fur border, and is finished with a black satin sash trimmed with fringe. Black velvet hat with lace ends. **Fig. b:** Hungarian suit. The trowsers, short dress, and paletot are of black velveteen, trimmed with kimmer. The trowsers are pleated and bound at the ankle. Round hat with black velvet revers, trimmed with an ostrich feather and velvet rosette. Gloves of Danish leather trimmed with fur. High boots with fur trimming. **Fig. c:** polonaise trowsers and paletot of dark blue cloth trimmed with gray Astrakhan. Gray Astrakhan muff and boa. Toque of dark blue cloth trimmed with Astrakhan. High boots trimmed with fur. **Fig. d:** dress of garnet cloth. The under skirt is trimmed with a flounce, and the upper one is looped up in the manner shown in the illustration. Paletot and muff are of garnet cloth trimmed with rabbit fur. Black velvet hat with ostrich feather. High Russian boots.

Harper's Bazar, 1869; signature, Anais Toudouze.

Harper's Bazar double-page plate, 1879; signature, Anais Toudouze.

Harper's Bazar, 1880; signature, A.T.

In 1848, an English wood engraver named Henry Carter, age 27, came to America. As a boy he showed a talent for art, but his father did not encourage this particular leaning. Smuggling some of his drawings to London through the mail—on the off chance they might be used—Carter signed another name: Frank Leslie. The drawings were published and Frank Leslie began a career that eventually brought him to America. When Jenny Lind began her tour in 1850, Carter arranged with Barnum to illustrate programs for her concerts, and followed her around the country. By 1854, the Frank Leslie publications had arrived. His earlier training led Leslie to create innovations in rapid production of engravings. For the fashion plates, he, as Godey, used the plates produced by the Capewell and Kimmel Company.

The 1850-1853 black and white fashion drawings in *Harper's Monthly Magazine* were engraved by Lossing-Barrett; beginning in 1853, fashions were sketched by Voigt (del) "from actual articles of costume furnished by G. Brodie"; W. Roberts, Sc, was the engraver. Voigt

continued as a fashion artist, with Roberts presumably the engraver (although not noted on all the drawings), until the fashion drawings were discontinued in 1864. Voigt also supplied fashion drawings to *Godey's* in 1864, with the identical description, "drawn from actual articles . . . . "

Thomas Illman, born in England, worked in London as an engraver in 1824. Arriving at New York about 1830, he formed the firm of Illman and Pelbrow, which became Illman Sons about 1845. The firm engraved portraits for both New York and Philadelphia publishers, but also must have used the production line process for fashion plates. *Peterson's* fashion plates were produced by the Illman firm from the early 1860s into the 1890s.

Harper's Bazar, through their arrangements with *Der Bazar*, displayed the work of many European artists—particularly the remarkable Colin sisters of England: Anais (Toudouze), Laure (Noel) and Heloise (Leloir). Their work began to appear in the late 1840s in Europe; the work of Anais continued until the 1890s. Unfortunately, information about their personal lives is rather

Harper's Bazar, 1880; signature, A.T.

Harper's Bazar, 1880; signature, H.C.

Ladies' Own Magazine, 1873.

Bow Bells (English), 1872; signature, Colin.

DUST CLOAKS FROM WORTH *(4.9.1892, cover)*. A travelling cloak large enough to envelop the dress beneath is of satin merveilleux with glossy surface that repels dust. It is shot in copper shades, and the light lining is of fancy surah. The second protective outfit has a long jacket with a skirt to match made of Silesienne, a ribbed fabric of light weight and self-colored. The peculiar feature of the jacket is a Watteau fold down the front as well as the back.

Harper's Bazar, 1892; signature, A. Sandoz.

WORTH EVENING AND CARRIAGE CLOAKS *(4.7.1894, p. 280)*. Every accessory of a fashionable woman's toilette is extremely important. Comfort and grace are alike to be considered in the style of wraps she chooses for day or evening. These should sometimes be splendid and harmonious, rich and exquisite in fabric and adornment. Beauty should go beautifully when she drives abroad. The first of these elegant cloaks is used by Parisiennes for the carriage in afternoon drives as well as for an evening wrap. It is made of black satin, trimmed with black marten fur on a part of the cape, and descending like a round boa down the front. The small cape of full pleats is attached to a yoke covered with white guipure mounted on black net. The coiffure, in Empire style, is called Sans Gêne by Lenthéric. It is waved close to the head, and has a large puff and small curls in the back surrounded by strands of pearls. A tiara and aigrette complete the coiffure. A second cloak of black satin is in bell shape, and is embroidered in stripes from the collar to the foot all around. An opening on each side forms a sort of sleeve, which is very long, and is bordered with fur, as is the entire garment. The lining is of pink satin on which white lace is applied. The evening hood from the Maison Virot is of white satin covered with black and white lace trimmed with white satin ribbon.

Harper's Bazar, 1894; signature, A. Sandoz.

sparse. Anais was born about 1822, married August Toudouze, and was a widow about 1863. Her daughter, Isabelle, followed the mother's footsteps, becoming a fashion artist. Heloise married Jean Baptiste Auguste Leloir, a French historical painter. Two sons were born of this marriage, Louis Auguste (1843) and Maurice (1853), each of whom followed in his father's footsteps.

Anais' work usually carried the signature Anais Toudouze, although some are merely signed "A.T." Heloise signed her work in a variety of ways: the initials H.C. alone, Heloise, Heloise Colin or Heloise Leloir. The work of all three sisters appeared in many of the European fashion magazines—French, English and Italian—and of course, in *Harper's Bazar*.

It is the work of Anais that probably is the most unusual. Her earliest fashion plates are characterized by either one or two figures. In 1879, there appeared in *Harper's Bazar* a double-page plate containing 14 figures, the plate itself measuring 13 inches by 19 inches. A plate of 1880 contained seven figures, portraying masquerade costumes for children ranging in age from five to 15 years.

Through the pages of *Harper's* also passed the work of one of the best of the European fashion artists—Adolph Karl Sandoz. Research has turned up very little information about him, other than that he was born in Odessa, Russia, in 1845 and later transplanted to Paris. His illustrations for the House of Worth are strikingly beautiful and completely different from the style of Anais.

The fashion plates of America evolved slowly. In the beginning, the prints were politely stolen, re-engraved and issued as "Americanized Fashions." These were hand-colored in homes—a cottage industry—or in small workshops set up for the purpose. The next step came in the purchase of the plates from England or France, with the printing and coloring done on a production line basis in America. Graham obtained his plates in the completed stage from France, and it is likely that other periodicals of the time did the same. In the establish-

ments of firms like Capewell and Kimmel, Lossing-Barret and the Illman Bros., complete production probably was done in the American shops. This was the *Golden Age of Engraving*, when the art and skill of engravers was of paramount importance—not that of the original artist. It is equally plausible that some of the artists of the day may not have wished to sign their work. This may have been regarded as "hack work" used to fill in the lean days.

Voigt might then be classified as the first American fashion artist, since his were among the first of the signed plates published in the 1850s. Madame Demorest emerges as a fashion artist in an even stronger sense, since she created both the fashion and the drawings. Those in her employ also were a combination of designer and artist. Their transposition of French fashion into wearable American styles gave the Demorest plates an undeniable Yankee stamp. While the detailing of the clothing is finely done, the modelling of the face and body line do not have the beauty of expression so noticeable in many of the *Bazar* plates, particularly in the work of Sandoz.

In retrospect, it becomes obvious that the skill of the fashion designer or artist had to be equal to that of the engraver, and vice versa. When like talents were merged, the resulting fashion plates were things of true beauty.

As the gay 90s approached, so did the *Golden Age of Illustration*. The photo engraving process began to pull the engraver from his throne and put the artist in his place. The beautiful American women drawn by Charles Dana Gibson, Henry Hutt, Guernsey Moore and Harrison Fisher began to predominate the magazines of the era. These too were replaced when the camera finally created the living personification of La Grande Pandore who had travelled from the Hotel de Rambouillet in Paris, spreading fashion news in her wake.

(See Appendix I for chronological listing of fashion plate publishers.)

PARIS RECEPTION GOWN *(12.25.1897, cover).* An exceedingly effective gown is made with a skirt of velvet trimmed with a deep flounce of point-lace, which is appliquéd on to the velvet, and is bordered by a band of sable fur. The sleeves are of velvet, tight-fitting except just at the top, and made with deep cuffs edged with fur. The body of the waist is entirely of white lace, in blouse effect, made over a satin lining, with a high-stock collar, and flaring side pieces of velvet covered with lace. The distinctive part of the gown is a collar which is cut out in front and back like a square-neck dress, and this has a long stole end which broadens towards the foot of the skirt and hangs the entire length. The hat worn with this gown is a large soft velvet toque the same shade, trimmed with two long ostrich plumes fastened with a rhinestone buckle. Just under the brim to the left side is a rosette of satin ribbon with another rhinestone buckle.

Harper's Bazar, 1897; signature, A. Sandoz, Derbier.

THE COSTUMES

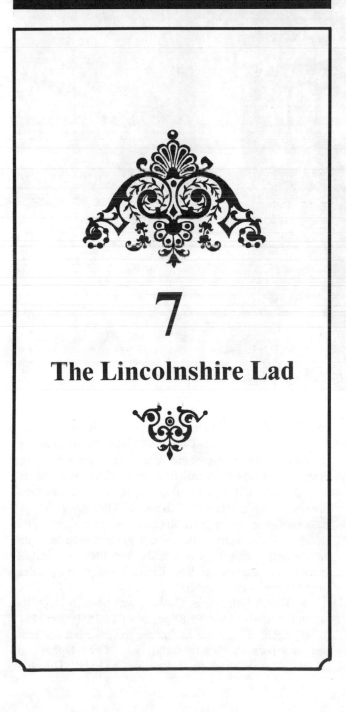

7

The Lincolnshire Lad

The young man of 12, intensely studying the 16th Century portraits in the museum, scarcely would have rated a second glance from a casual observer. The year was 1837, and Victoria had been seated on the throne of England. Slight of build, completely absorbed, there was little to indicate that one day this young man would be a despotic ruler in a cosmopolitan court, a confidant to an Empress, and King of the Victorian fashion world.

His father had gambled away the family inheritance and the boy was forced to begin work at the age of 11 in a printer's shop. His mother became a charwoman to help sustain the family. Even at that age, Charles Frederick Worth knew that his fortune lay elsewhere and he finally persuaded his mother to allow him to go to London. Here he secured work in the mercantile establishment of Allenby's, learning the fine art of salesmanship and acquiring an understanding of and a feeling for fabrics. Later he worked in other shops, including Swan and Edgars at the corner of Picadilly. Evenings were spent in museums and art galleries, always absorbing line, color and fashion.

Destiny intervened again, and Charles Worth followed the inner voice that told him to go to Paris. There he arrived at the age of 20, with about 25 dollars in his pocket. Starting in a small dry goods store, Worth finally went to work for the firm of Gagelin, which handled dry goods, but also was the first to handle cashmere shawls and ready-made coats. While there, he met a shy young girl who was employed as a "demoiselle de magazin"—the word mannequin had not yet been invented. It was not too long before the shy girl, Marie Vernet, became Mrs. Worth. After their marriage, Charles began to design special gowns for her that were greatly admired by the Gagelin customers.

From this interest Charles conceived the idea of a dressmaking department. Gagelin completely disagreed with this approach, but Charles was a very persuasive man. At the time, dressmaking was not much of an art. Customers could buy their material and trimming at a firm like Gagelin's. If the customer was a good seamstress, the clothing was made at home; otherwise, a local dressmaker was employed. Charles pointed out the obvious advantage to the firm of not only selling the material and trimming, but of completing the entire gown to the customer's satisfaction as well. Gagelin finally relented and, before long, the dressmaking department was extremely successful.

The Lincolnshire Lad (Brooklyn Museum, see Credits)

Charles seized the opportunity to create new designs, and as each new model was completed, Mrs. Worth wore the gown in the showroom. Modelling was always a trying task for Mrs. Worth because she was extremely shy—and remained so for the rest of her life.

By 1851, the reputation of Charles Worth was firmly established. The long hours spent in museums and galleries, the many years of handling fabrics, the creative talent—all combined in his success. At this time, his attention was turned to an early interest: He had been particularly enchanted with the passementerie work he had observed in the museums. In 1855, he decided to combine jet beads with braid and introduced jet passementerie trimming on clothing. It was met with hostility and opposition, pronounced too heavy and too showy. The fashion-minded ladies had no way of know-

ing that Charles Worth was endowed with a generous supply of persistence. Two years later he tried again, introducing jet passementerie as trimming—this time using it in a more restrained fashion. His idea was accepted, and for the next 50 years, jet was the principal ornament of coats and dresses. The price of jet passementerie was a little high at the time Worth first made his Gagelin models, so he also employed lace and embroidery. Lace, jet's first real competitor, was initially rejected just as jet had been. Twenty years later, jetted lace was high fashion.

The Worth's first son, Gaston, was born in 1853; the second son was Jean Phillipe, born in 1856. By 1858, Worth decided the time had come to strike out for himself and formed a partnership with Otto Doberg of Sweden, established at 7 Rue de la Paix. The first

House of Worth, from Harper's Bazar, 1874.

couture house was born, and the doors swung open for the parade of elegance that continued for more than 50 years.

In 1859, Worth was appointed dressmaker to the French Court and to Empress Eugenie. Eugenie often has been depicted as a fashion leader. In truth, she was quite hesitant about adopting any new fashion. Worth and the Empress argued on this point more than once, with Eugenie winning and one of the ladies of the court wearing a new design. After it was accepted, Eugenie would adopt the fashion.

Worth set himself to the task of improving the quality of French materials. Under his prodding, the French mills began to produce higher quality brocades, velvets and silks. A part of the motive for such prodding was that shoddy materials did little or nothing for the kind of clothes Worth created. A deeper reason lay in the loyalty Worth felt toward France. The French fabrics must be the best!

By the 1860s Worth's salon was firmly established, and he introduced the practice of showing completed gowns on live models to prospective clients. By 1867, the House of Worth was the mecca for the wives of American businessmen and merchants attending the International Exhibition in Paris. The future Mrs. Frank Leslie had appeared at the Exhibition wearing a $20,000 purple gown from the House of Worth. And no American woman worth her salt would dream of returning home without a trunkful of Worth gowns.

Worth disliked the bonnet, or cabriolet, as intensely as he liked jet. The bonnet shaded the face and hid most of the hair, which Worth considered a woman's crowning glory. So he designed a special hat for Mrs. Worth, that showed the face and hair and persuaded her to wear it to the races, over her usual protests. When the carriage of the Princess de Metternich drew alongside Mrs. Worth's carriage, and the Princess complimented Mrs. Worth on her charming hat, a new fashion was born. Worth also succeeded in killing the crinoline in 1866 or 1867 by inventing the gored skirt that fit at the waist and flared out. By 1870, fashion was going full steam ahead, and Worth was King of it all.

The following is a description of the great couture house, from the 1870s:

"As you entered the House of Worth through the double swinging glass doors you are greeted by a reflection of yourself as others see you, for a long mirror faces the entrance door. As you turn into the long corridor, you see it is lined with settees. At the end, to the right, are rooms for fitting dresses, inspecting colors by gaslight, private consultations and afternoon tea. At the opposite end, to the left, are the show rooms and the King's audience room. There are four rooms, each

linked to the other, well lighted with long windows looking out over the Rue de la Paix. Scattered throughout the rooms are counters covered with goods, wall cupboards with doors ajar and goods stacked upon the shelves, chests of drawers half open, revealing more material. On a door post is pinned a bunch of scraps of every color, above a card with some jumble of words not decipherable. There are few chairs as people who go to Mr. Worth's are not expected to sit down; but there is not much standing room either, for Mr. Worth is holding court. Clustered about him is a group of men and women—American, English, French, Russian and Spanish. And there stands Mr. Worth in the center, dressed in a blue flannel sack coat, buttoned across his person, brown trousers, a turn down collar and a crimson scarf, all shabby."

The Lincolnshire lad was king of fashion and head of the first couture house in the world. This was the period of the Second Empire—l'epoque de Worth—which suddenly crashed in the Franco-Prussian War—not discouraging Worth at all.

Charles knew that while wars come and wars go, fashion endures. Women did without many things during war time, but as soon as the conflict was over, fashion again was uppermost in their minds. Europeans might not have had the money to buy, but Americans were great spenders. When they went to Paris they intended to buy beautiful, frivolous things, not practical goods. English women rarely were wasteful; the French women had economy in their bones, but the Americans —"Ah, they have great faith in me," said Worth, "with figures I can put into shape and money to pay the bills."

In 1874, both Gaston and Jean became permanent members of the Worth firm, Gaston as business manager and Jean as designer and salesman. Jean had started out to be an artist, studying under Corot. But the dressmaking business was in his blood, just as it was in his father's. Charles Worth was not prudent in handling money, but Gaston was, making outside investments that eventually helped to create a source of wealth for the Worth family. Contrary to what may have been believed, the dressmaking business itself did not make Worth's fortune.

The American fashion periodicals of the day usually contained columns reporting the latest in Paris fashions; in the columns of *Harper's Bazar, Woods Household Magazine, Peterson's Magazine* and others of the 1870s to the 1890s, the name of Worth appeared again and again, to the exclusion of all others. It seemed as if only one fashion house existed in Paris. One short article in the personal column of the November 8, 1879, issue of *Harper's Bazar*, demonstrates clearly the regard held for the House of Worth:

WORTH'S SEAMLESS DRESS *(2.20.1892, cover).* Seamless corsages have found such favor that a seamless dress has been produced by Worth's creative brain. This dress of elastic wool, as ladies' cloth or crépon, drawn smoothly over a fitted waist lining of silk, and covering a bell-shaped skirt of silk. Cutting the cloth bias facilitates matters in these dresses, as it then clings more closely when stretched around the waist, and also furnishes greater fulness in the skirt. Seams that are absolutely necessary are concealed by trimming, and the dress is fastened invisibly, usually on the left side. The dress illustrated gives the effect of a princesse back, with round waist front. Blue cloth is the material used, with sleeves and panel of narrow bias folds applied on a maize yellow ground. The yellow contrast, now so fashionable with blue, is further given in open gold passementerie. Later in the season the fur band can be replaced by a fine ruche of gold ribbon. Changeable taffeta silks are used by French modistes for the waist and skirt lining of wool dresses, with a pinked balayeuse of the gay silk at the foot.

House of Worth, from Harper's Bazar, 1892.

AN EVENING GOWN FROM WORTH AND COIFFURE FROM LENTHÉRIC OF PARIS *(4.15.1893, cover).* This elegant ball gown of *ciel*-blue damask has a distinctive style given by its rich trimming of embroidered lace and pearls. A charming design of pink chrysanthemum petals is brocaded on delicate blue ground. The corsage is pointed in front, and is trimmed all around the low neck with white tulle and lace gracefully festooned. A double garland of pearls mounted on tulle with crystal pendants starts on the bust and curves to the right at the waist, where it is fastened by clasps in the form of St. Jacques shells. The damask skirt has similar garlands of pearls and crystal festooned diagonally across the front above a flounce of embroidered lace, which drops down the left to join the side of the damask train. At the foot of the skirt, which is gored in umbrella shape, a deep flounce of embroidered lace is added under a ruche of tulle. The hair is parted in the middle and drawn back in large waves to a high coil, and is ornamented with twists of pearls.

House of Worth, from Harper's Bazar, 1893.

EVENING GOWN FROM WORTH, COIFFURE FROM LENTHÉRIC OF PARIS *(3.17.1894, cover).* This superb gown is of very light *ciel*-blue satin bordered with black fur. It is further enriched with bead embroidery in iris designs. The pointed waist is draped across the bust, and has a jabot falling between branches of embroidery done on the satin. Fur shoulder-straps complete the square décolleté. Short puffed sleeves of dotted mousseline de soie are under a ruffle of beaded satin. The graceful skirt falls in godet pleats, and is trimmed with embroidery and fur. The coiffure is without any ornament, a looped tress at the back extending above the top of the head giving a pretty profile. The fan is of black lace figures appliquéd on tulle.

House of Worth, from Harper's Bazar, 1894.

"A Paris correspondent of the *Chicago Times* says that if a lady tourist from America wishes to hold a realization of what is supposed to be very high style in dress, she has only to go to Worth's and ask for Miss Mary. An English brunette will respond to your summons—a brunette with large blue eyes and a slender figure and mien of blended reserve and dignity. She will take your orders with the air of a queen and will move to execute them with the step of a duchess. She is the very incarnation of style; that mysterious quality is diffused throughout her being, from the summit of her dark tressed head down to the tip of her shapely slipper. Were she clad in a tow bag, fastened around the waist with a hempen cord, she would impart to that garb a subtle air of elegance. She is always arrayed in some one of the latest creations of the presiding divinity, and whatever it may be, she looks well in it. Her smooth, pale complexion defies the effects of color and she can wear pale green or golden yellow with equal impunity. Ruffs cannot deform her throat, and puffed sleeves are powerless to impart an ungraceful carriage to her arms. She moves in a tie back like a swan and carries a train with the unconscious ease of a mermaid. She is never flustered or put out, or impertinent or familiar. Stout matrons and skinny maidens beholding the charm and grace of her appearance, ascribe it all to her gown, whereof they straightway order duplicates making guys of themselves in the process. She is the worthy Prime Minister to the acknowledged King of Fashion."

At the same time that Worth's name appeared constantly in the fashion columns, jet was given equal attention. Over and over, column after column, appeared jet passementerie, jet fringes, jet rain, jetted lace, jet embroidered stockings, jet buckles, jetted silk, jetted hat aigrettes, jet nail heads, and so on. After its hostile rejection in 1855, jet rode a wave of popularity that reached tidal wave proportions by 1890.

Despite the disruptions of the Franco-Prussian War (the House of Worth had closed its doors during the war) and the establishment of a new fashion center in Vienna, Worth's empire held its own. With the promotion he was getting from American fashion magazines, his continued high standing in the French Court and his position as leader in the fashion world, Worth became downright picky about his clients and liked only those who could show off his gowns to good advantage. One of his favorites was the statuesque Queen Margherita of Italy; one fashion columnist described her gowns as "poems—or, rather, works of art—in silk and satin."

Another favorite was Lily Langtry, who launched new Worth fashions by virtue of her fame and magnificent figure. Lily made her acquaintance with the House of Worth during her first visit to Paris in 1880 with the Prince of Wales—the future King Edward VII—who bought her a complete Worth wardrobe. In 1883, Lily returned to Paris to study dramatics under Francois Joseph Regnier and bought a dazzling wardrobe from Jean Worth. Jean was to become an even greater designer than his father and an astute businessman under the guidance of Gaston. He personally checked each design and completed gown to make sure it was perfect, for he firmly believed that each Worth gown was an advertisement of itself. Worth's clothes were expensive and Lily bought 50 dresses from Jean. Lily, whose brains equalled her beauty, paid only a fraction of what the gowns would have cost anyone else, in exchange for giving Worth program credit. When she returned to America in 1894, 40 trunks of Worth clothes accompanied her and Worth's first jersey costume, a blue pleated skirt with tight fitting bodice and red sash, was introduced by Lily.

In Washington, on May 1, 1893, President Grover Cleveland pressed the button of a golden switch and Chicago's Columbia Exposition was opened officially; Mrs. Potter Palmer appeared that day in a Paris gown of heliotrope and black crepe, studded with jet, nailheads and threaded with gold passementerie. Her hat was of heliotrope velvet with black ostrich tips and jet trimming; her white broadcloth wrap was lined with white satin.

The only cropper that Jean Worth ever hit was Eleanora Duse, the dramatic Italian actress that Eva La Gallienne called the "Mystic of the Theater." Eleanora was a naturally beautiful woman, but she cared little for gussy-up clothes and fancy hair do's for personal use. At the age of 40 she looked 60; her streaked gray hair was simply tucked back and her street clothes had a shabby look. Jean first met Duse in 1896; he was the designer for her stage clothes and taught her the art of stage make-up. But away from the stage and Jean's influence, Eleanora would slip back to a nondescript manner of dressing. In spite of this, Eleanora and Jean remained friends for many years.

In their private lives, the senior Worths lived in a large brick red chateau at Suresnes—about half an hour from Paris by train—along with their sons, Jean and Gaston. At home, Charles puttered about in old clothes—a rusty brown jacket and a battered straw hat without a crown—while Mrs. Worth might appear in a white satin short-sleeved dress striped with bands of black velvet, trimmed with lace; long suede gloves reaching almost to her shoulders, with diamonds half hidden here and there in the lace. They would dine in a large greenhouse, amidst a forest of palm leaves, tree ferns, variegated verdures and fantastic flowers. Here, too, was a

YACHTING COSTUME FROM WORTH *(7.7.1894, cover).* The French yachtswoman's taste in dress differs greatly from that of her English sister. The latter wears a trim tailor-made gown of serviceable serge or linen, with a blouse and reefer of the simplest shape, and a sailor hat or yachting-cap like those worn by men. Something more fanciful both in stuffs and style is preferred by the Parisian. This gown is of white repped wool finely dotted all over the surface, a non-shrinkable

stuff not heavier than serge, but far more effective. It is made with a Directoire basque of very simple shape, with revers of white moiré, and clasped by a moiré belt. The very full skirt is bordered with three bands of the wool, each edged with a narrow piping of white satin. A charming little collet to add when stiff breezes blow is of white wool of the gown. A Parisian touch is given in the thick waving puffs of white mousseline which trim the shoulders, and the full collar of mous-

seline around the neck. The Virot hat is of white straw wholly covered with white lace. Two *choux* of light green velvet are set under the brim. On each side of the crown are white and black birds with wings and tail pointed upward, as if preparing for flight. The low shoes are of white canvas, and loose large gloves of heavy white kid complete the attractive ensemble.

House of Worth, from Harper's Bazar, 1894.

FRENCH PROMENADE COSTUME FROM THE MAISON WORTH *(7.11.1896, p. 588).* The material used in this gown is changeable moiré taffeta, the colors of a pigeon's throat. The skirt has box-pleated front while the back is in godets. The waist is trimmed most effectively with white mousseline de soie and a pleating of appliqué lace. A broad belt of white satin ribbon is finished at the side with a soft bow, while the collar matches the belt. The parasol is of chiné Pompadour taffeta trimmed with lace to match that on the waist of the gown, and the dainty hat of réséda straw is trimmed with flowers, a tuft of ostrich feathers, and a stiff lace aigrette.

House of Worth, from Harper's Bazar, 1896.

large and well kept aviary. "When I am at a loss for a new idea in color blending," said Worth, "I go and watch my birds and find it."

For all his wealth and exclusive clientele, Worth frequently was referred to as the "man milliner," and his clients refused to accept him as their social equal. "Really, my dear, he is just my dressmaker!" But Worth had the last laugh, for he knew full well why women purchased his gowns, and had summed it up pretty well in 1871: "Women dress for two reasons: for the pleasure of making themselves smart, and for the still greater joy of snuffing out the others." And for the pleasure of snuffing out others, the fashion-minded ladies paid Worth a pretty penny.

When Worth opened the doors of the House of Worth there were only 158 dressmaking establishments in Paris; by 1898 there were 1,939. While the couture houses of Europe grew, the face of America began to change. The industrial revolution was hitting high gear and, in the ready-to-wear industry, the emphasis was on everyday wear. High fashion was left to the Continent. The home sewing machines whizzed along and dress patterns became available. Those ladies who were handy in the beadwork department could make their own jet passementeries and fringes following instructions in the periodicals. Or they could purchase jet trimmings from the large department stores. Solid jet fringes, one to ten inches deep, ranged in price from $1.50 to $21.00 per yard. Fringe aprons of chenille and jet cost between $15.00 and $35.00 each. Ornaments or medallions with jet beads ranged in price from 35 cents each to $3.75 each. Jet tassels cost 50 cents each to $5.00 each. Jet novelties, as they were produced, cost from $2.50 each to $50.00 each.

At the close of the Franco-Prussian war, the House of Worth was flooded with orders from both England and America. One sage piece of advice that had been given to Marshall Field when he opened his new store in Chicago in 1879 was to import Worth gowns. These would insure the success of his women's clothing department. Those women who could afford to travel to Europe purchased their gowns in Paris; those who could not patronized the stores of Lord and Taylor in New York or Marshall Field in Chicago. The 1896 Marshall Field catalogue carried a special section devoted to the fashions of the great European haute couture houses.

Worth's passion for jet had been taken up by other European designers as well. Some of the gowns presented in the Field catalogue were the creations of Jules Bister, Berlin; Debenham & Freebody, London; Ulman & Straus, Frankfort; A. Izambard, St. Petersburg—each featuring trimmings of jet.

The use of jet reached its peak during the gay 90s—dresses, cloaks, hats, shoes, stockings sparkled with it. Jet ornaments were worn in the hair; jet jewelry and jet buttons completed the costume. The jet craze crested at the time of Charles Worth's death in 1895. Perhaps there could be no more fitting memorial to the passion and persistence of the Lincolnshire lad.

Jean Worth, carrying on the House of Worth after his father's death, was invited to display at the Paris Exposition in 1900, but was given only a small, dark corner. Here he installed a Louis XVI drawing room, and made it a composite picture of British life, from court costume to maid's uniform. Jean had learned well from King Charles, for his exhibit stole the show and was one of the chief drawing cards at the exposition.

The Gibson Girl

As the century turned, the life style of American women began to change. Instead of being spectators, they were more and more becoming participants in the world about them. Ms. America was engaging in active sports; education was opening new fields and women could no longer be hampered with the frills, furbelows and ornamentation of previous years. The hour glass figure was out and a slimmer, tailored look became the new standard of fashion. It was time for a change, and the person who helped to usher jet out the door was a pen-and-ink lady named Penelope Peachblow, whom history now remembers as the Gibson Girl.

Using his beautiful wife, Irene, as the first model, Charles Dana Gibson created a vision of loveliness that was to become the ideal for American girls to copy. Tall, slender, beautifully proportioned and simply gowned, Penelope moved through Gibson's drawings for *Life* magazine in the 1890s. The skirt and shirtwaist became one of her hallmarks for day wear; her evening dress was of elegant cut with little adornment—no hint of jet was to be found. The Gibson Girl captured the fancy of American women, who copied her mannerisms and fashion which, incidentally, were well suited to the new life style of American women.

From Paris, the names of other designers were coming to the attention of fashion-minded women: Paul Poiret, who began his career with Worth and designed the first women's suits; Lucile, Molyneaux, Doucet, Madame Vionnet, who helped banish the corset; Paquin, Patou, Redfern and Drecoll. But the clouds of World War I were gathering, and by the time the war had run its course, Paris couture houses had lost supremacy, never again to wield the power that had marked the House of Worth.

During the 1920s jet enjoyed a brief revival, but never with the same popularity that it had enjoyed before. In

*Penelope Peachblow—The Gibson Girl. Upper right: 1975
pewter necklace made from a 19th Century mold.*

Dress of the 1920s in black chiffon with beading on tunic in crystal, pink and red.

place of the heavy silks, brocades and velvets, the lighter silks and crepes were used, which simply could not support the heavy passementerie. Jet ropes were used as evening gown straps; smaller, lighter-weight beads were used in trimming skirts; occasionally a jet fringe of narrow width might appear. During this time, the *Ladies' Home Journal* featured the clothes of Paris designers, including those of the House of Worth. But now, the Worth designs received the same billing as the others.

At 70, Jean Worth, grayed but still keen and quick, was active in the business, but made no secret of his dislike for current fashions. To him they must have represented the nuts and bolts of clothing. Said Jean, "We are more artificial and less rich in harmony." To him, softened faces, fine curves, dignity of carriage, grace of movement and depth of expression were the essentials of beauty in dress. Jean's feelings were the bittersweet memories of an era that could never return. As a young boy, Jean had gone to the French Court with his father, and from a small gallery his eyes had been dazzled by the beautifully gowned Eugenie and her ladies-in-waiting. Small wonder that the 1920 fashions had no appeal for him.

Destiny had put Charles Worth in the right place at the right time. The New World was ripe for the plucking, and as fortunes multiplied the money to buy the beautiful and the frivolous in Paris was at hand. The House of Worth and jet passementerie remained linked together for all time as representative of the era of plush. While the Victorian ladies could not have been very comfortable in their layered, overladen clothing, they were the epitome of "Elegance," and have left behind a rich legacy for us to remember.

The End of an Era

In 1927, the *Ladies' Home Journal* began a series of articles written by Jean Phillipe Worth—"Dressing the World of Fashion for a Century." Four installments appeared, then publication suddenly ceased. The death of Jean Worth had cut short the intimate story of Charles Frederick Worth, as remembered by one of his sons.

In 1962, the Brooklyn Museum, New York, gathered together a collection of original Worth gowns; some were from their own collections, others were loaned by individuals and other institutions. The dresses exhibited began with a ball gown of the 1860s and continued through an evening gown c. 1908. Their publication of the exhibition supplied the end of the story begun in the *Ladies' Home Journal*. The author expresses her appreciation for the permission granted by the Museum to complete the story:

Both Gaston and Jean passed away in the "twenties," Gaston's son, Jean Charles, became designer for the house; son Jacques continued in his father's role as business administrator. Gaston's grandsons sold out their interest in the couture house after World War II; the name then was used by a London wholesale firm. *Parfums Worth*, originally established by Jean and Gaston around 1900, continued in the 1960s with Roger Worth serving on the Board of Directors.

When the House of Worth was sold, and its operations transferred to London, historian James Laver collected what remained of the records and sketches, delivering them into the safekeeping of the Victoria and Albert Museum. Costume buffs of the 21st Century will find there the rich treasure left by Charles Frederick Worth, King of Fashion in the Victorian era, a man of his times.

THE COSTUMES

8

Nimble Needles

In definition, passementerie means trimmings, especially of braids, cords, gimps, beads or tinsel. Passement, or passemaye, was the name by which trimming made of gold or silver braid or ribbon originally was known (from the Orient). A great deal of it also was made in Italy; by the 16th Century, the Parisian passementiers were sufficiently numerous to form their own guild. Within the guild were groups of specialists—those who worked on dress, furniture, uniforms and the upholstery of carriages. By the 18th Century, the French passementiers had developed a high level of skill. As Charles Worth developed the use of jet passementerie, cord or braid was used to form the basic design, to which the hundreds of small black glass beads were sewn by hand.

Cole's Encyclopedia of Dry Goods, published by the Root Newspaper Association in 1900, gives a very clear account of the production of passementerie work:

"The passementerie used in the United States is for the most part imported from Germany and France, being produced by the cheap, peasant labor of those countries. The raw material used in the manufacture embraces narrow silk gimp, ribbon, braid and cord, jet, metal, pearl and glass beads, together with buckram, satin and various kinds of cloth for the foundation work. The beads are obtained chiefly from Coblentz in Prussia and Venice in Italy, the other materials required being mainly of local production. The design for the passementerie is first drawn on a thick strip of paper and given to the worker. The latter then sews on narrow silk cord, gimp or buckram, according to what the foundation of the trimmings is to be, and the gimp or buckram firmly tacked at different points to form the figure. When this is accomplished, the basting threads are cut and the design is complete upon the foundation. In the next process comes the slow work of ornamentation by beads, if the passementerie is to be of this character. Over the design is sewed black or colored beads in rows sufficient to cover up the foundation completely. After this the worker forms wheels, fans, crescents, etc. in artistic designs within the open spaces of the pattern, the entire work being done by hand. When wound upon boards and wrapped with attractive papers the goods are ready for shipment."

Victorian passementerie beadwork is characterized by drops, fringes and tassels with two or more ornaments often looped together by festoons of beads. The fringes were to grow in length and be called jet rain.

A second method employed in this era was *Tambouring*, in which the fabric was embroidered directly, not by needle and thread, but by means of a small, sharp hook. The pieces of clothing were cut first and sent to the tambour workers for the beading. The material was stretched on a round frame, wrong side up, with the pattern traced on the wrong side of the fabric. The beads reached the tambour worker prestrung; the beader would fasten the thread (matching garment color) to the string holding the beads and transfer all beads to the new thread. The right hand held the tambour hook above the wrong side of the material; below the frame, the left hand slid the beads, one at a time, presenting the thread to the hook as it was driven in and out of the fabric. Between each bead, the hook brought the thread to the upper surface (wrong side) of the fabric, and each bead became securely fastened to the underside, or the right side of the fabric. On the wrong side of the fabric, a chain stitch could be seen.

Cole's Encyclopedia adds another interesting note: "In Germany, the bulk of the work is produced in factories employing 50 to 200 peasant women, the latter receiving from 25 to 40 cents per day. The finest work, however, is made by the peasants in their own homes, from patterns and materials supplied them by the factories. The most skilled workers on fine passementerie seldom earn more than 75 cents per day."

Throughout the 19th Century, in western Europe, a constant struggle for power raged between the royal houses of Prussia, Austria and Russia. Poland eventually was swallowed up by all three; Bohemia became the spoil of Austria. The peasants were shifted from pillar to post in a bewildering change of boundaries. Small wonder the New World beckoned to them with a siren's call. Sadly for them, Victorian America had not yet acquired the heart to match its progress. Instead of finding the pot of gold, the immigrants exchanged one kind of misery for another—crowded into tenements, working long hours in the mills, factories or mines. Or, equally as bad, they were caught in the trap of the sweater.

The sweater acted as a contractor for manufacturers, farming the work out; whole families crowded into one room, slept, ate and worked in that room. One 1870 periodical described a sweater as a "dealer in human endurance. To him it matters little how small the price of the work, if he can secure enough of it; he looks out for his own pay first, and pays the workmen whatever is left." And all too often, the sweaters skipped town just before payday. For the women and children who strung the endless beads to form the sparkling beaded ornaments, life often was bleak.

Whether the work was passementerie or tambour, the conditions under which it was produced were the same—in Vienna, Paris or the tenements of America. The beadwork shops truly were sweatshops where the women worked long hours for little pay. If the fashions changed and beading was less popular, the beaders could easily starve. Worth had 1,200 people in his employ, and surely a great number of these must have been the beadworkers. And if Worth had work rooms that could have been termed sweatshops, he was no different from many other business houses who also maintained them. Worth's fondness of passementerie also could have been motivated by his genuine love of the craft and the wish to keep it alive. When the Franco-Prussian War closed the doors of the House of Worth, there was genuine concern for the welfare of his workers: "How were they to live?"

The American garment industry was beginning to grow, and for the women who worked in it, the conditions were among the worst in the country. Wages were as low as $2.00 and $3.00 per week, with a work week ranging from 60 to 70 hours in lofts that were firetraps. In 1871, New York's A.T. Stewart Department Store had a loft where the dresses were made for sale in the store below. Marshall Field's new store had the fifth floor set up as a work room where 300 women made dresses and the sixth floor was utilized as a cloak, fur and lace factory. Some employers even required the seamstresses to furnish their own needles and made deductions for damaged materials.

The voice of Sarah Hale, speaking out for women, had been stilled in 1879. But two new voices were waiting in the wings; the first was that of Mary Harris Jones, later nicknamed "Mother Jones"; the second was that of Bertha Honore Palmer, Mrs. Potter Palmer.

Mother Jones

As the great Chicago fire turned the city into ashes in 1871, crowded along the shores of Lake Michigan with thousands of other refugees, Mary Harris Jones sat stunned as she watched the fire sweep Chicago. Now a 41-year-old widow, all that Mary possessed was gone. In 1861, she had stood by helplessly as her husband and each of her four young children had died in the yellow fever epidemic that swept through Memphis, Tennessee. Mary would always remember the cry of the death cart driver: "Bring out your dead." From Memphis Mary had gone to Chicago where she opened a small shop following her early training as a dressmaker. As Chicago was being rebuilt, Mary began to attend the meetings of small groups of workmen attempting to form labor unions. Before long, Mary was swept into the movement and became a labor organizer. For the next 50 years, her life was an endless repitition of travelling about the country on jerk water trains and sitting in dirty railroad depots; her life was threatened many times and she was shot at more than once.

Her special loves were the miners of the land and the helpless children who were forced into labor at the tender ages of six and seven. How she acquired the nickname "Mother" is not known—perhaps the miners—perhaps the children gave it to her. A small, feisty Irishwoman with silver gray hair and a prim Victorian bonnet, Mary spoke out against the evils of the mines and the sweatshops. When challenged on this point, Mother replied; "I have never had a vote, and I have raised hell all over this country! You don't need a vote to raise hell! You need convictions and a voice!" Mary did not believe in men's rights or women's rights, she believed in human rights (more on Mother Jones in chapter 12).

Bertha Palmer

A much younger pair of eyes watched the same fire in 1871. A new bride, standing on the porch of her home on the outskirts of Chicago, Bertha Palmer realized that the newly built Palmer House, her wedding present, was going up in smoke, along with the other buildings her husband had built in the downtown sections of Chicago. The Potter Palmers were probably broke!

Potter Palmer was a man of determination, and as Chicago was rebuilt, he rebuilt the family fortune. Twenty years later, Mrs. Palmer used the gentle technique of Sarah Hale, speaking in a soft voice, to persuade the governing board of the Columbian Exposition to erect a Woman's Building. Here would be shown the many contributions women had made in building both America and Europe. Travelling at their own expense, the Palmers went to Europe where Mrs. Palmer persuaded the queens of royal houses to send to the exhibition the best examples of the handiwork and talents of their women.

Her efforts were just beginning. Shocked by the exploitations of the less fortunate members of their sex, a small but dedicated group of middle class and wealthy women organized the Women's Trade Union League for the purpose of helping secure better working conditions and higher wages for those women who had been treated unfairly for so long. Mrs. Palmer loaned the strength of her high social position in helping the milliners organize, often inviting the shopgirls to the Palmer Castle for luncheon and strategy meetings.

In the East, Mrs. O.H.P. Belmont applied her energies to the league, and gave a benefit tea for women's suffrage at Marble House. It would be very easy to characterize these women as "do-gooders" who had nothing else to do with their time. For these, or any woman, to speak out, even those who had great wealth and unassailable social positions, was not easy. That some did, even at the risk of ridicule by members of their own sex, is a tribute to their personal courage. Not all women of that day were fooled by the sentimental drivel that filled the magazines.

What would the effect have been had Sarah Hale, Mother Jones, Godey, Bertha Palmer and the Demorests formed a theatrical troupe? Sarah would have written the lines for Bertha. Ellen Demorest would have designed the beautiful gowns for the equally beautiful Bertha to wear and dazzle the audiences while softly speaking the eloquent words of Sarah. Godey and William Jennings Demorest would have been the advance ballyhoo men. Mother Jones would have been riding shotgun (with an empty gun, of course), all the while reminding Sarah not to forget the little children. Collectively, they might have been able to advance the cause by 20 years. No, Penelope Peachblow was not the sole reason for the change in clothing styles.

The lovely jet passementeries that now remain speak mutely in their own special language. The shimmering facets mirror not only the great balls and parties, but reflect as well the suffering and misery of the tenement, the horror of the firetrap lofts, the bewilderment and agony of the European peasant leaving all that was familiar and dear for a New World.

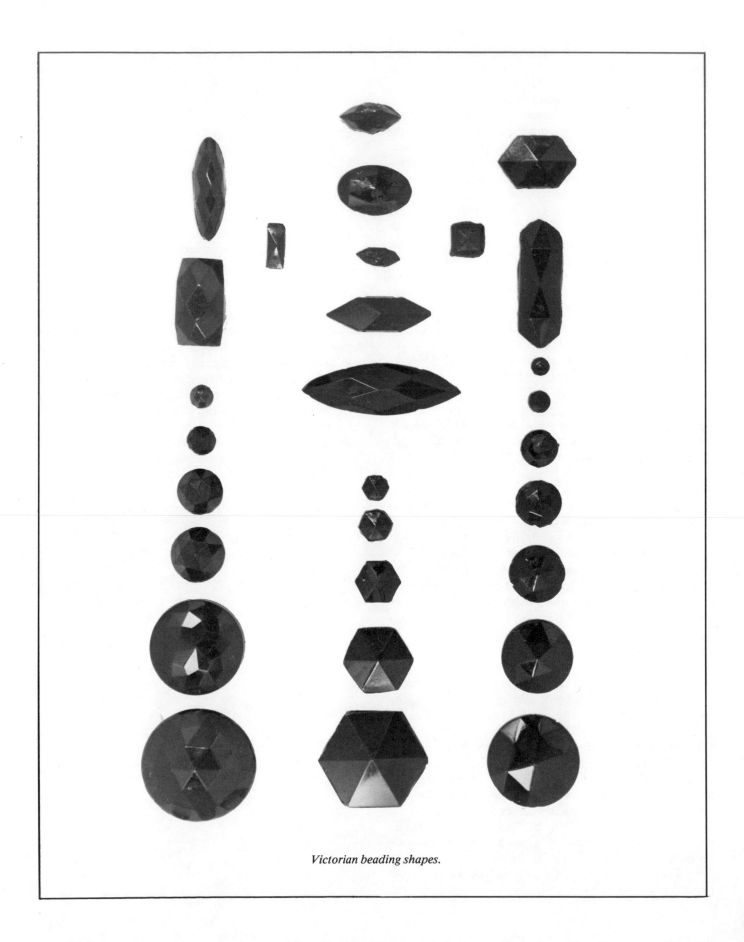

Victorian beading shapes.

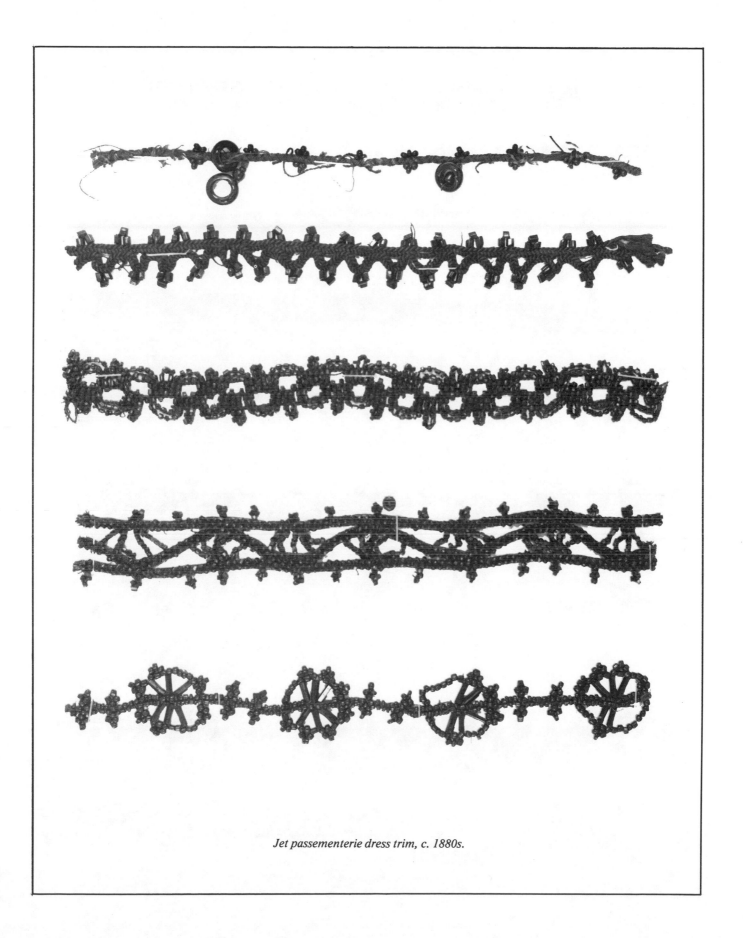

Jet passementerie dress trim, c. 1880s.

Evelyn Swenson

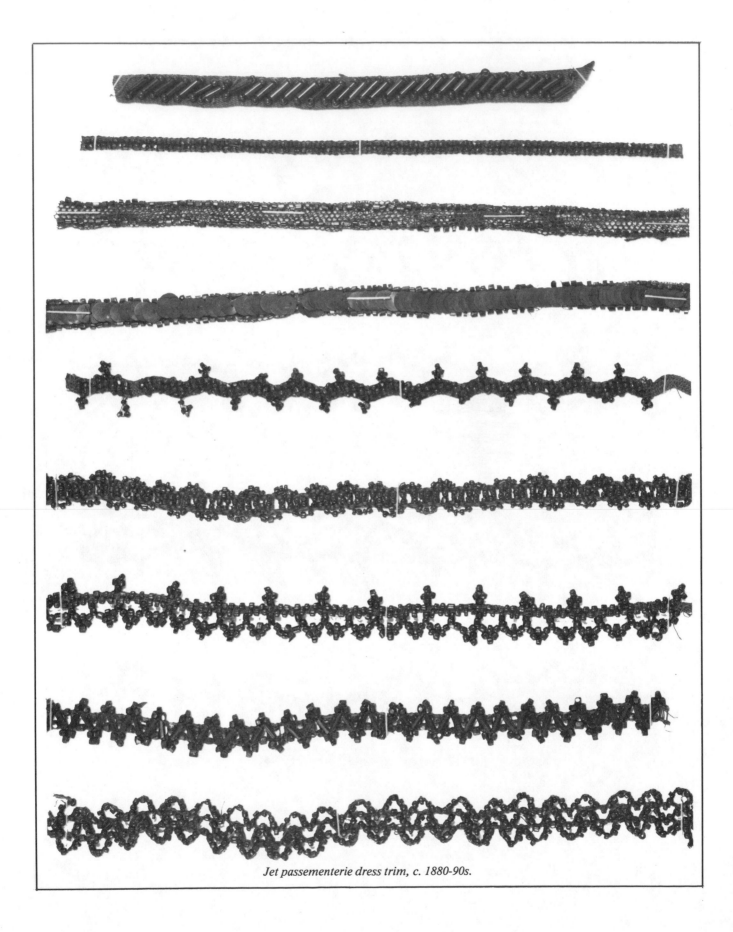

Jet passementerie dress trim, c. 1880-90s.

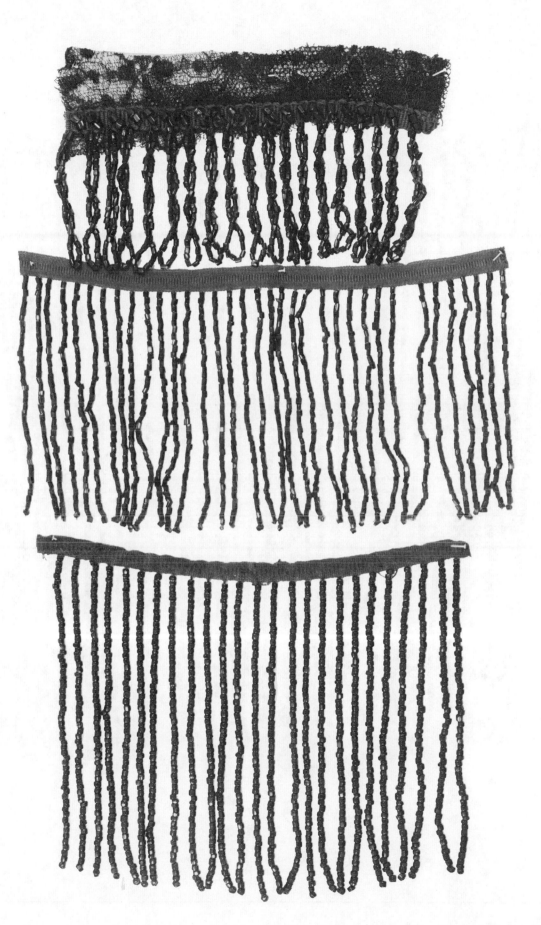

Jet rain fringe, c. 1880-90.

Ten-inch jet rain fringe, c. 1880-90.

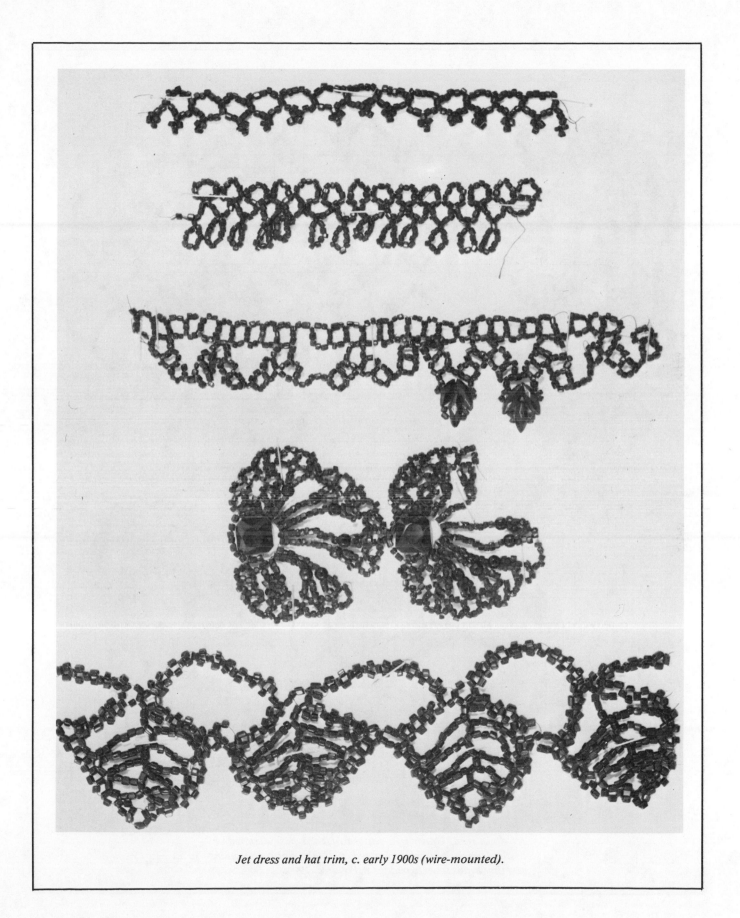

Jet dress and hat trim, c. early 1900s (wire-mounted).

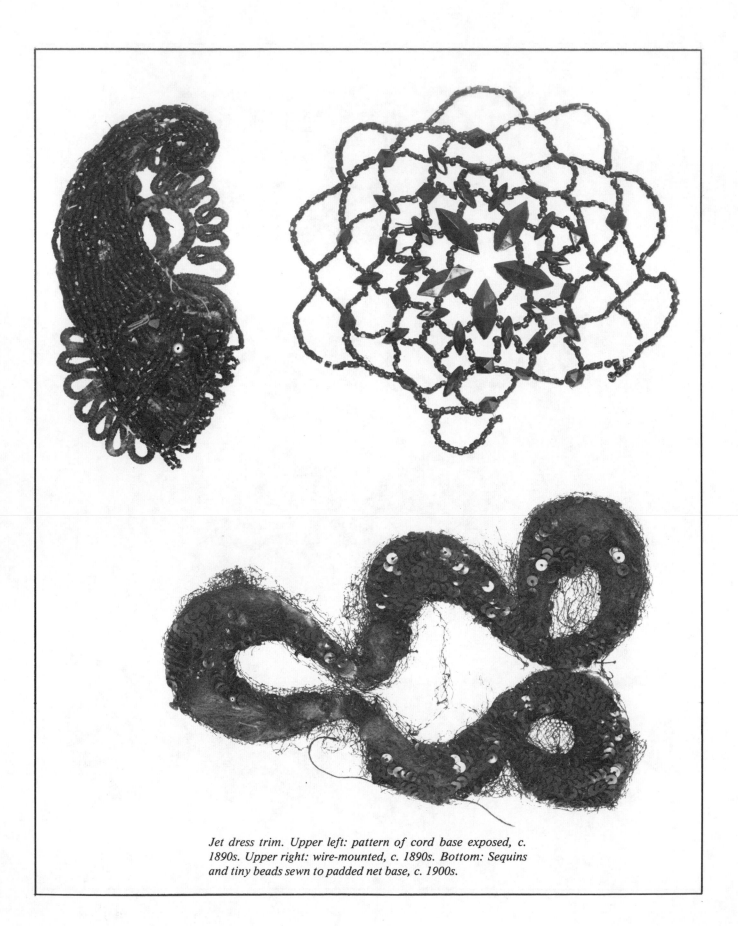

Jet dress trim. Upper left: pattern of cord base exposed, c. 1890s. Upper right: wire-mounted, c. 1890s. Bottom: Sequins and tiny beads sewn to padded net base, c. 1900s.

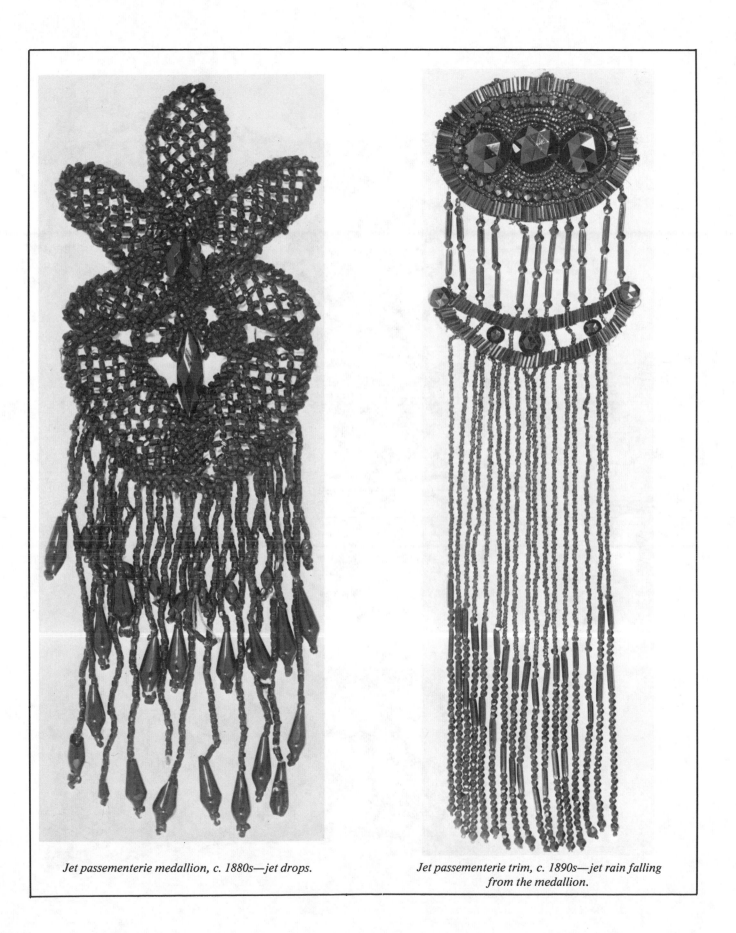

Jet passementerie medallion, c. 1880s—jet drops.

Jet passementerie trim, c. 1890s—jet rain falling from the medallion.

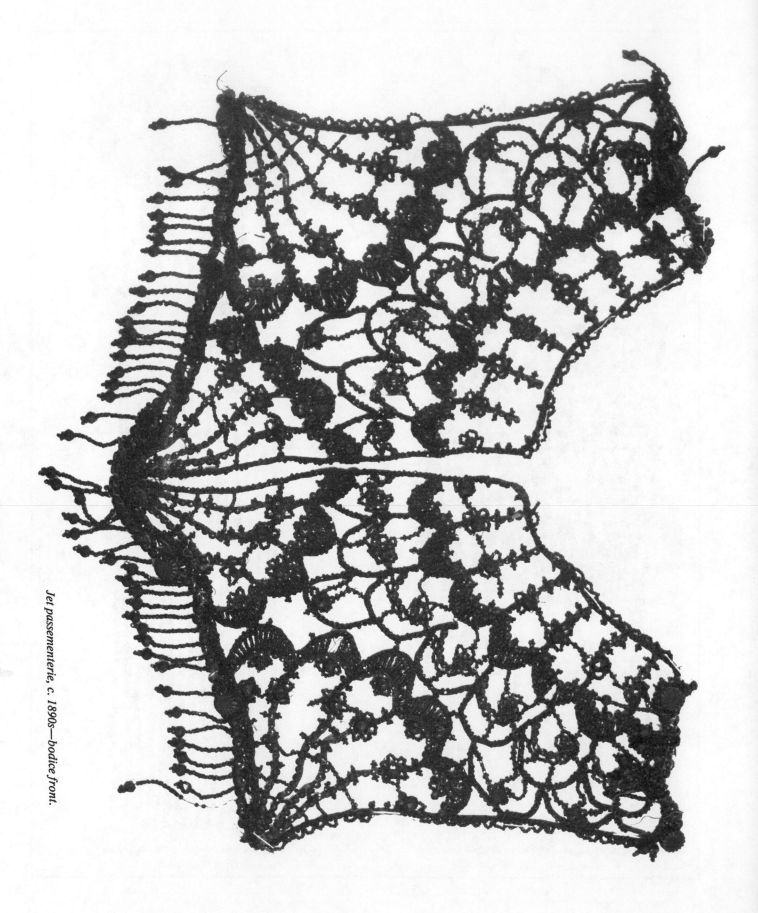

Jet passementerie, c. 1890s—bodice front.

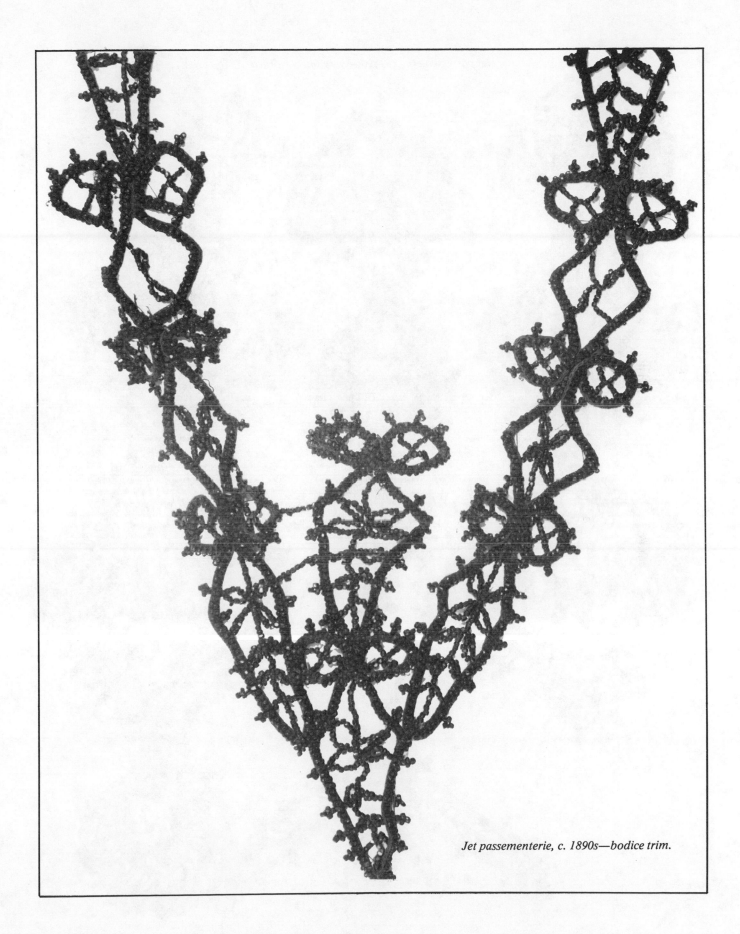

Jet passementerie, c. 1890s—bodice trim.

Jet passementerie, c. 1890s—very finely worked.

Jet passementerie, c. late 1890s—jacket lapel trim.

*Multi-colored beads on a collar from the evening gown worn
to the Inaugural Ball of Grover Cleveland.*

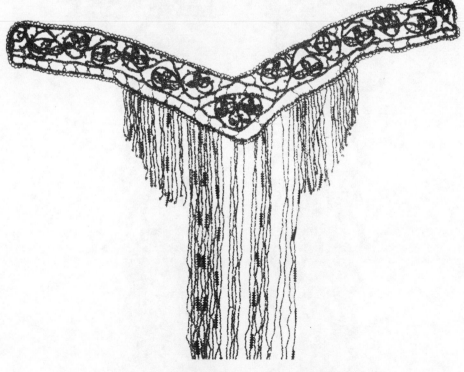

*Jet passementerie, c. 1880s—opera cloak trim with the
jetted train at the back.*

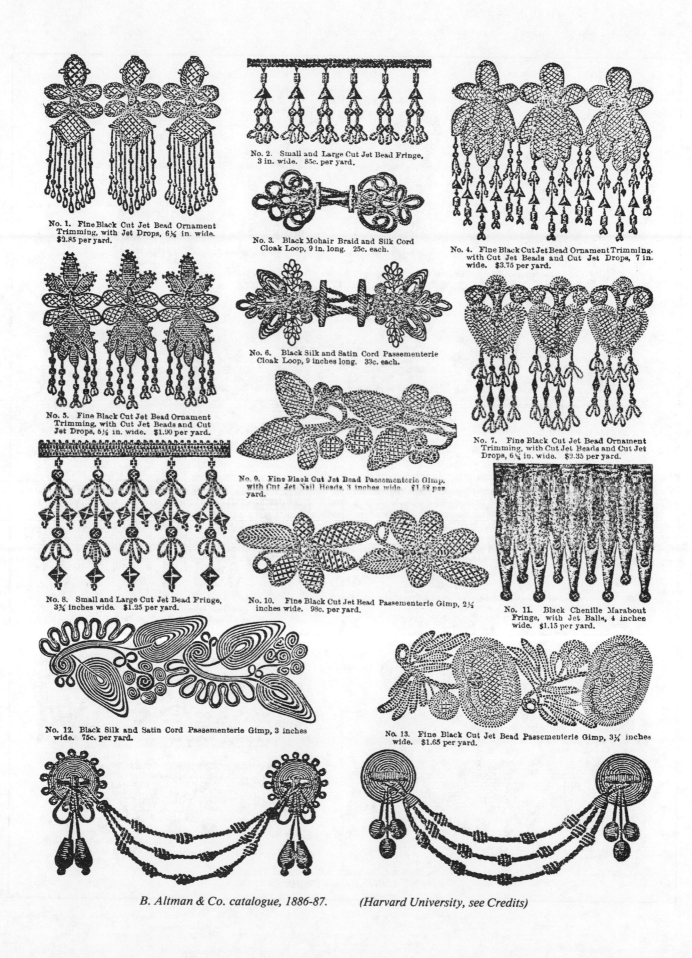

No. 1. Fine Black Cut Jet Bead Ornament Trimming, with Jet Drops, 6½ in. wide. $2.85 per yard.

No. 2. Small and Large Cut Jet Bead Fringe, 3 in. wide. 85c. per yard.

No. 3. Black Mohair Braid and Silk Cord Cloak Loop, 9 in. long. 25c. each.

No. 4. Fine Black Cut Jet Bead Ornament Trimming, with Cut Jet Beads and Cut Jet Drops, 7 in. wide. $3.75 per yard.

No. 5. Fine Black Cut Jet Bead Ornament Trimming, with Cut Jet Beads and Cut Jet Drops, 6½ in. wide. $1.90 per yard.

No. 6. Black Silk and Satin Cord Passementerie Cloak Loop, 9 inches long. 33c. each.

No. 7. Fine Black Cut Jet Bead Ornament Trimming, with Cut Jet Beads and Cut Jet Drops, 6½ in. wide. $2.35 per yard.

No. 8. Small and Large Cut Jet Bead Fringe, 3¾ inches wide. $1.25 per yard.

No. 9. Fine Black Cut Jet Bead Passementerie Gimp, with Cut Jet Nail Heads, 3 inches wide. $1.59 per yard.

No. 10. Fine Black Cut Jet Bead Passementerie Gimp, 2½ inches wide. 98c. per yard.

No. 11. Black Chenille Marabout Fringe, with Jet Balls, 4 inches wide. $1.15 per yard.

No. 12. Black Silk and Satin Cord Passementerie Gimp, 3 inches wide. 75c. per yard.

No. 13. Fine Black Cut Jet Bead Passementerie Gimp, 3¼ inches wide. $1.65 per yard.

B. Altman & Co. catalogue, 1886-87. *(Harvard University, see Credits)*

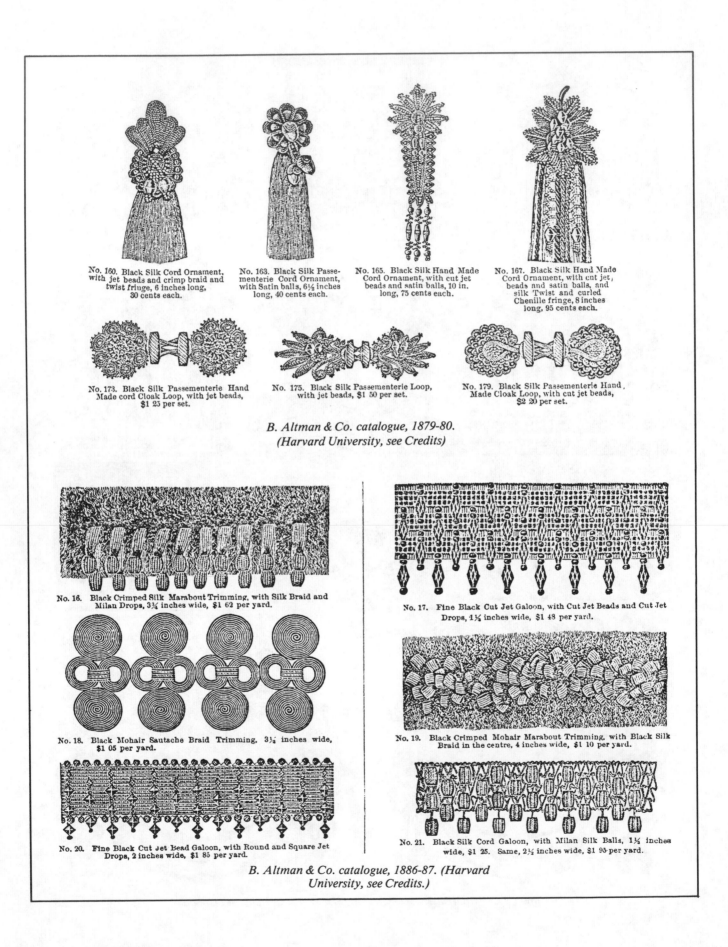

No. 160. Black Silk Cord Ornament, with jet beads and crimp braid and twist fringe, 6 inches long, 30 cents each.

No. 163. Black Silk Passementerie Cord Ornament, with Satin balls, 6½ inches long, 40 cents each.

No. 165. Black Silk Hand Made Cord Ornament, with cut jet beads and satin balls, 10 in. long, 75 cents each.

No. 167. Black Silk Hand Made Cord Ornament, with cut jet, beads and satin balls, and silk Twist and curled Chenille fringe, 8 inches long, 95 cents each.

No. 173. Black Silk Passementerie Hand Made cord Cloak Loop, with jet beads, $1 25 per set.

No. 175. Black Silk Passementerie Loop, with jet beads, $1 50 per set.

No. 179. Black Silk Passementerie Hand Made Cloak Loop, with cut jet beads, $2 20 per set.

B. Altman & Co. catalogue, 1879-80.
(Harvard University, see Credits)

No. 16. Black Crimped Silk Marabout Trimming, with Silk Braid and Milan Drops, 3¾ inches wide, $1 62 per yard.

No. 17. Fine Black Cut Jet Galoon, with Cut Jet Beads and Cut Jet Drops, 1½ inches wide, $1 48 per yard.

No. 18. Black Mohair Sautache Braid Trimming, 3½ inches wide, $1 05 per yard.

No. 19. Black Crimped Mohair Marabout Trimming, with Black Silk Braid in the centre, 4 inches wide, $1 10 per yard.

No. 20. Fine Black Cut Jet Bead Galoon, with Round and Square Jet Drops, 2 inches wide, $1 85 per yard.

No. 21. Black Silk Cord Galoon, with Milan Silk Balls, 1½ inches wide, $1 25. Same, 2½ inches wide, $1 95 per yard.

B. Altman & Co. catalogue, 1886-87. (Harvard
University, see Credits.)

LACE AND FRINGE CRAVAT BOW.
For description see Supplement.

Harper's Bazar, 1880.

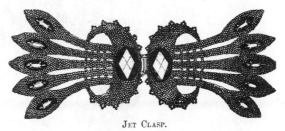

JET CLASP.

Jet Clasp.

BEAD clasps such as that illustrated are used in various sizes to ornament the vests of dresses and the fronts of mantles. The surface of the mould is covered with fine cut beads, and ornamented with larger faceted plates.

Harper's Bazar, 1884.

B. Altman & Co., 1886-87. (Harvard University, see Credits)

No. 211. Cut Jet Dog Collar, 98c., $1.25, 1.35, 1.75, 2.00.

No. 210. Fine Cut Jet Dog Collar, with Pendants, $2.45, 2.75, 3.50, 4.25.

No. 209. Long Beaded Jacket, with Bodice and Dog Collar attached, $13.50.

No. 214. Jet Pompadour, with Fine Cut Jet Pendants, $2.90.

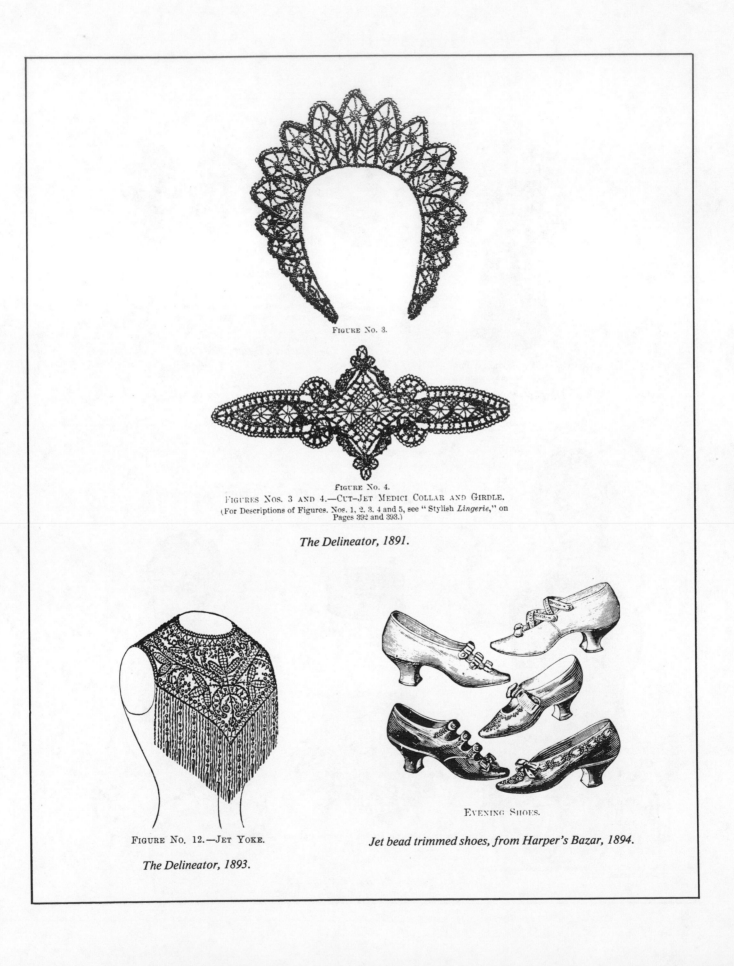

FIGURE No. 3.

FIGURE No. 4.
FIGURES NOS. 3 AND 4.—CUT-JET MEDICI COLLAR AND GIRDLE.
(For Descriptions of Figures. Nos. 1, 2, 3, 4 and 5, see " Stylish *Lingerie*," on
Pages 392 and 393.)

The Delineator, 1891.

FIGURE No. 12.—JET YOKE.

The Delineator, 1893.

EVENING SHOES.

Jet bead trimmed shoes, from Harper's Bazar, 1894.

Jetted lace Van Dyke collar, c. 1880s.

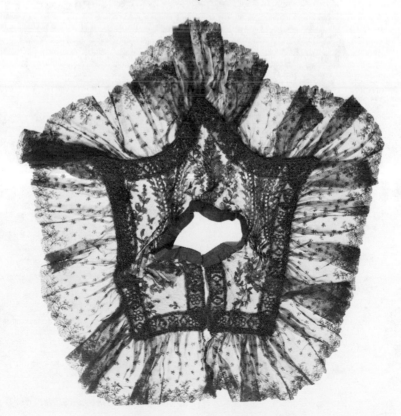

Jetted black lace Bertha collar, c. 1880s.

Jetted lace pelerine (shoulder cape), from Harper's Bazar, 1881.

A mantelet of black Ottoman silk has netted shoulder pieces with jet and plum-colored beads, a dark red surah lining showing through the mesh and front trim to match. Hat is of black Marquise over red surah, trimmed with jet and plum beads and buckles to match, from Demorest's Magazine, 1886.

Satin cloak trimmed with lace and jet passementerie, from Harper's Bazar, 1882.

Garments trimmed with jet passementerie;
left, 1885; right, 1883.

*Jackets trimmed with jet passementerie:
top, lace; bottom, satin; from The Delineator, 1890.*

A SEASIDE TOILETTE *(6.6.1891, cover)*. This charming picture tells its own story. Summer is come, and the graceful *mondaine* quits the delights of the town for the invigorating breezes wafted over the sunlit water. It is afternoon, yet her gown is of the simplest, fashioned exquisitely by Worth from soft fine wool of the pale tint of Persian lilacs. The rich *camail*, or bishop's mantle, is of cream-colored *molleton*, a soft flannel-like cloth. It is studded with jet cabochons, and has a yoke of jetted passementerie, with rain fringe of jet, and a flaring collar finished with a lace ruff. The hat, from the Maison Virot, is of transparent black horse-hair popularly known here as Neapolitan braid. Rose-colored ribbon is added in erect wired loops at the back, and long streamers hanging down the waist. A parasol of white chiffon mousseline completes the toilette.

Jetted cloak by Worth, from Harper's Bazar, 1891.

A WORTH CLOAK SEEN IN THE LOUVRE
(3.4.1893, cover). This cloak is a recent creation which is given character by its great simplicity of form and the arrangement of its
decorations. In ensemble it recalls the styles
of old Egyptian costumes, and for this reason
the artist has not feared to commit the
anachronism of placing the elegent woman
who wears it beside the sculptured sphinx in
the Musée du Louvre. It is made of fine mastic

wool. Two bands of pearl-gray velvet forming
scarfs on each shoulder start at the waist in
front, and extend just underneath the
shoulder-blades in the back. This velvet is
embroidered with many rows of jet beads and
cabochons. Below the scarf numberless
threads of jet fringe fall in festoons on the
skirt, and return to be attached in the back.
The large sleeves, very bouffant on the shoulders, are pleated below on flaring sleeves of

wool widely bordered with silken Persian.
The high collar, also of Persian, has turned-
over points in front, and very effective revers
are added below. Below the revers is a very
large ornament of jet, and a pendant of jet
butterflies completes this superb cloak. The
little capote is of gold braid surrounded by
black lace gathered all around. A large
dragon-fly with wings of blue and gold is its
charming ornament.

Jetted cloak by Worth, from Harper's Bazar, 1893.

*Skirts trimmed with jet passementerie, from
The Delineator, 1893.*

*From The Delineator: left, 1896 dress of green and black vel-
vet trimmed with mink and jet; right, 1893 dress with jet rain
fringe on bodice and sleeves, and jet cabachons above each
row of ruffles.*

Jet beaded bell or lamp pull, c. 1890s.

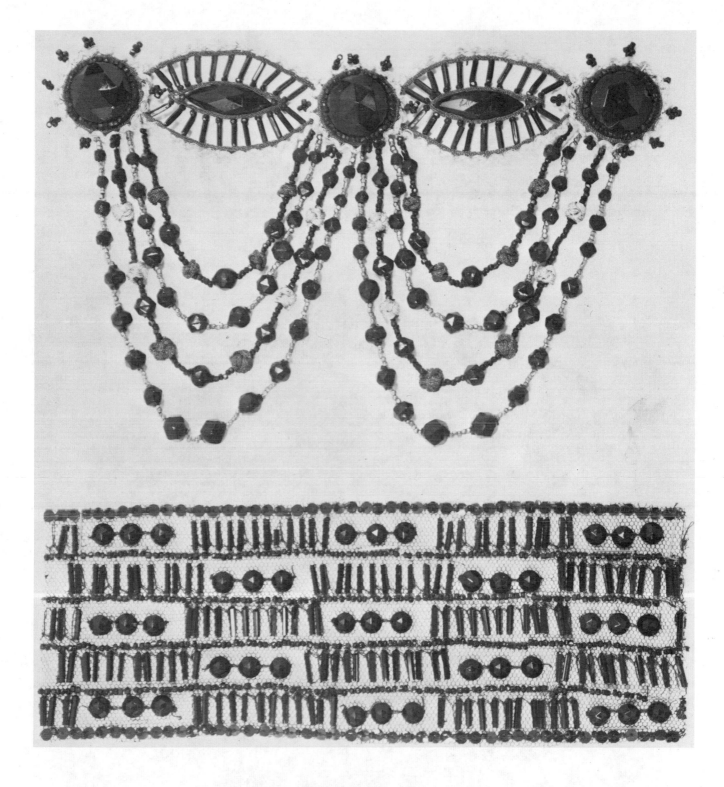

Jet lamp shade trim, c. 1900s.

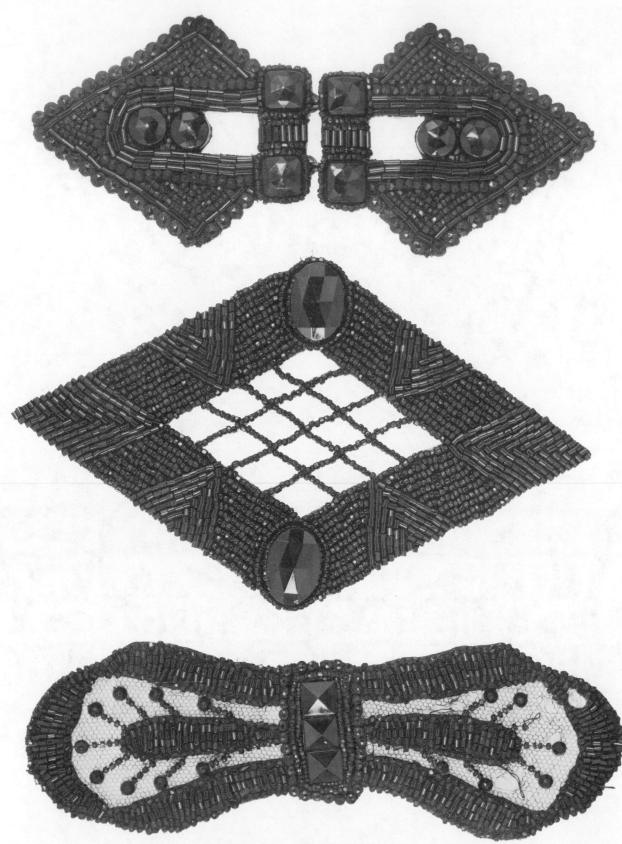

Jet beadwork, c. 1920s, geometric shapes.

THE COSTUMES

9

Ostrich Feathers

The use of ostrich feathers, or plumes, on clothing and hats reached its peak during the late 1880s and 1890's. Historians feel the industry had its origin in immigrants from France, later through French immigrants from Haiti, who were adept at making artificial flowers and feathers. The industry centered in New York City, and as early as 1840, about 10 manufacturers were listed there.

In their natural state, the ostrich feathers were not full enough to be truly elegant. Three or four of the natural feathers usually were combined to produce one luxuriant plume. To combine the feathers, the quills, except the lowermost sections, were cut away; the feathers then layered one on top of the other, and finally all were sewn or tied together. Wire often was inserted to give the plume a pleasing curve. The actual small feathers, or "flues," then were drawn over a square edge to produce the curling effect.

Ostrich tips were made in the same way, using three feathers. The popular "willow" plumes were made by tying the flues stripped from one feather to the ends of the flues of the base feather. An even more luxuriant willow plume was made by stripping a third feather and tying the flues to the ends again of the second set of added flues, thus making the flues three times their natural length.

Little wonder the ostrich flocks were decimated so badly that government action was needed to prevent their extinction.

Plumes of the 1880s.

Black silk and feather fan, c. 1880s.

CUSTOMS AND CRUSADES

10

For the Sad Times

Historians often deride the mourning practices of the early United States as a "grisly business," and describe Victorians in particular as being excessively morbid. Their customs merely were a reflection of both English and European customs, many of them centuries old.

In Europe, before newspapers were invented, obituary notices were served by means of a Death Cryer; dressed in black livery, painted and embroidered with skulls and cross-bones, the cryer strolled through the town broadcasting the news of a death. The custom of black attire in the family might have originated in the fashion whim of Anne of Brittany. All the queens of France had worn white when in mourning; Anne decided to wear a black gown on the death of her husband, King Charles VIII in 1515. The barbe headdress worn by the nuns of the late 15th and 16th Centuries was adapted to mourning, particularly the pleated bib which covered the chin.

In England there was a black bed that travelled from one family to the next, complete with black sheets and hangings. Another English custom was that of draping the entire house in black. Mirrors and pictures were covered with black cloth. The window shutters were slightly bowed and tied together with black and left for months.

In the colonies, mourning women sat in front of the pulpit, and the hearse was drawn by black horses with scutcheons on their sides and death's heads on their foreheads. Carriages were hung in black and black liveries were worn. Even the bottoms of the shoes were blackened, and the funeral often took place at night, which added to the somber tone. Widows of the 1600s wore white widow's caps with black dominoes, which were a type of hood or veil, also worn as an ecclesiastical garment.

Proper funeral etiquette could be very costly, for mourning dress, and gloves in particular, frequently were provided by the family or through the will of the deceased person. At a Boston funeral in 1736, over a thousand pair of black gloves were given away. The funeral expenses of a Baltimore citizen in the 18th Century included these sundry items:

Coffin
41 yards black crape
32 yards black tiffany
11 yards black crape
5½ yards black broadcloth
7½ yards black shalloon
8½ yards black
  Callamanco
16½ yards linen
3 yards shirting
3 dozen pairs men's
  black silk gloves
2 dozen pairs women's
  black silk gloves
6 pair men's cheaper
  black gloves
6 Pair Women's Cheaper
  black gloves
Black silk handkerchiefs
Mohair buckram
13 yards black ribbon
47 lbs. loaf sugar
14 dozen eggs
Ten ounces nutmegs
1½ lb. Allspice
21 gallons white wine
12 gallons red wine
10 gallons rum
Coffin furniture

As the prospect of the Revolutionary War loomed larger, the citizens of Boston decided upon a nonimportation system and a nonconsumption of articles upon which heavy duties were laid. They also decided to discontinue mourning dress; the only sign to be used was a piece of black crape about the hat, and a piece of black crape around the arm. It was further decided to give no other gloves than those of the manufacture of the colonies, with a distinctive mark upon them, such as a bow and arrow or pine tree.

It is difficult to fix the exact date when a band or armlet of black around the upper sleeve became an emblem of mourning. A black scarf was worn this way in the times of James I (1603-1625), so the colonists' choice of an arm band was not original. In Paris, 1793, the most popular entertainments were the bals a victime. To be admitted, one must have lost a relative by the guillotine. The dancers wore crape about the arm and danced gayly in honor of the deceased.

At the death of George Washington in December 1799, every American was asked to wear a badge of crape. Dwellings were hung in black; newspapers were black-bordered. Village churchbells tolled incessantly throughout the country. Mourning handkerchiefs stamped with Washington's portrait were sold in large numbers. Funeral pieces in memory of him appeared in china, glass, leather, marble, brass, bronze, pewter, paper, cloth and wood, with emblems and words of patriotic grief.

By 1800, there were strict rules governing the type of dress to be worn for mourning and the length of mourning periods for relationships extending to remote cousins and sister-in-law's sister. Bombazine and crape were to be used for the deepest of mourning. Bombazine was a fabric with a silk warp and a worsted filling. Since it was extremely irritating to the skin, it must have required considerable fortitude to wear the clothing for the extended periods of time required.

Crape (*Fr. crepe, OF. crespe, crinkled, from Lat. crispus, crisp*) was a thin fabric made of raw silk, which was twisted tightly without removing the viscous matter with which it was covered when spun by the worm. Woven as a thin gauze, the fabric then was dressed with a thick solution of gum, which in drying caused the threads to partially untwist, giving a wrinkled and rough appearance to the fabric. Its use as a mourning material originated in Bologna, Italy. Crape had one nasty habit; after being worn for any length of time, it began to turn a rusty brown, which may have been the reason for the phrase "widow's weeds."

On June 28, 1830, the Earl Marshal of England issued an order that all persons, upon the present occasion of the death of his late Majesty of Blessed Memory (George IV—Prinny), put themselves into decent mourning. The ladies were to wear black bombazine or plain black muslin and crape hoods, and to carry crape fans. It doesn't require much imagination to guess which fabric the court ladies chose.

By the mid-1800s, heavy crape was donned for every relative, and thick crape veils were worn for periods of several years. Often after the death of a cousin, uncle or aunt, unrelieved black would be worn for two or three years. Indeed, mourning clothes were a must in every woman's wardrobe.

One of the early tragedies of the White House occurred during the tenure of President Pierce (1853-1857). The Pierces had lost two of their boys in 1842 when Pierce was a United States senator. Before the inauguration of Pierce as president, the only surviving

*Jane Appleton Pierce in evening mourning dress of 1853.
(Smithsonian Institution, see Credits)*

Peterson's, 1888: crape-trimmed serge cloth jacket.

Crape trim with Kursheedt's standard mourning passementerie, from The Delineator, 1893.

Frank Leslie's Monthly, 1862: Dress of black silk with five small founces of crape. Second skirt is trimmed with narrow flounces of crape put on in festoons and ornamented with lozenges of crape. The sleeve is flowing and trimmed to correspond. Corsage is high and round, trimmed with silk bretelles, ornamented with crape. The tulle puff around the throat has undersleeves to correspond; black belt and buckle. Head dress is composed of black and white flowers and ribbon ornamented with bugles.

son, a 12-year-old boy, was killed before the eyes of his parents in a railroad accident. For evening wear, Mrs. Pierce had one gown made of black tulle embroidered with silver dots, worn over black taffeta. The dress was made in the fashion of the day, with a full skirt and tight bodice. With this, Mrs. Pierce wore a small black lace and net headdress trimmed with velvet, dull jet and gold.

Historians also have commented that a reader of *Godey's Lady's Book* during the Civil War would never have known there was a war going on, since there was rarely any mention made. When Sarah Hale assumed editorship of the book, Godey gave her a free hand with one exception: Religion and politics were tabu, and to Godey's way of thinking, the Civil War was tied into politics. One other explanation I would like to believe is that Sarah did not feel the need to remind the ladies more often than necessary. Leslie Publications were doing a splended job, thank you. Sarah knew the heartache well: She had lost her husband and one of her children at an early age. Across the land countless young wives were becoming widows, and mothers losing one, two, three or more sons in a bitter and tragic war. Some were never to know where their husbands and sons were buried; many Civil War cemeteries contain hundreds of unmarked graves. Sarah expressed her sorrow through poetry. Occasionally, Godey cast a veiled remark. But it may have been Sarah's belief that the women needed to think about something beside the war; the little octavo magazine contained short stories, poetry, needlework, fashions, which may have been one of the reasons that *Godey's Lady's Book* reached its highest circulation during the Civil War years.

Other magazines devoted full pages to the description of the proper type of mourning dress for "the unfortunate war in which our country is now plunged." Cashmere, paramatta and merino were used as the dress fabric, but the inevitable crape was still the only trimming destined for the deepest mourning. After the proper lapse of time, embroidery, passementerie, bands of black velvet and lace could be added. Jet passementerie was used widely for trimming, with chenille and gimp mixed in.

For evening wear, dresses of black tulle, or crape over black silk, were considered proper, as was black velvet. Jet trimming on the dress, jet buttons and jet jewelry were considered appropriate for evening wear. Mourning handkerchiefs were embroidered in black or violet, without lace trim.

For half mourning, moire antique and plain silk in black, gray and violet were considered proper. The flowers most appropriate for mourning were white roses, jasmine or violets without the natural foliage. If leaves were to show, they were to be of black velvet or

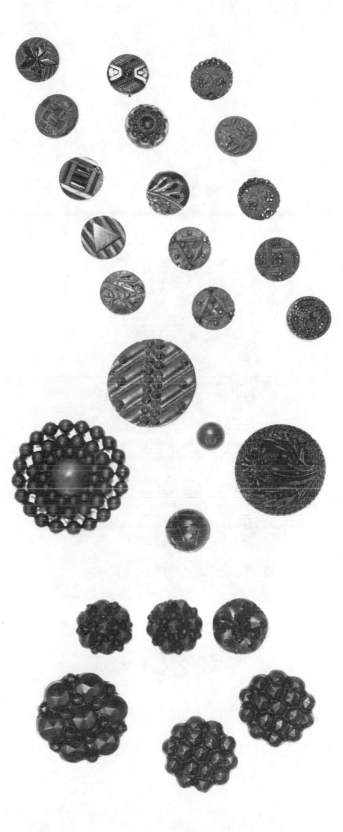

Black glass mourning buttons—dull and half dull finishes.

silk. Coiffures for ball and full evening dress consisted of wreaths of flowers, formed of mauve-colored velvet, with black velvet foliage, or white chrysanthemums with clusters of berries in jet.

There were specialty houses that carried nothing but mourning goods. Mrs. Jackson's store (par excellence) at 551 Broadway in New York carried black silk hats trimmed with English crape, embroidered with bugles and caught up with a chain of jet. The interior of one bonnet was "an exquisite melange of white roses, purple violets, black berries and wheat." The strings were of rich, wide black ribbon. "This bonnet may be worn in deep mourning, and it is certainly to reflect that the words 'deep mourning' no longer involve the necessity of actually looking repulsive, as in times past, when the hideous bombazine with its stiff crape folds were de riguer. Thanks to our transatlantic cousins we have changed all this now, and we think that the most skeptical on the subject of deep mourning will admit it is preferable to wear a becoming dress, and even admit to a display of taste and elegance."

Prior to the 1880s, the relationship between dirt and disease was not clearly understood, and society was helpless before the continued onslaught of plagues and epidemics that swept through the cities. Yellow fever, spotted fever and Asiatic cholera swept through the northern states, New York, Philadelphia, Washington, New Orleans, St. Louis and Detroit with amazing regularity. Nor were epidemics the only enemy. Tuberculosis also was rampant, along with small pox. Every summer saw entire households wiped out by typhoid fever. The death rate of children was three out of every five before they reached their fifth year, and the toll of men and women under 45 was proportionately large. Add to this the tragedy of the Civil War and the later horrors of the tenements and it is easy to see why the Victorians were on the morbid side—their morbidity was merely an expression of the grim reality with which they lived. And it is just as easy to see why the clothing of women was changing and becoming more ornamented. Black may have been becoming, but it also became very monotonous.

Proper mourning jewelry had its genesis in the cult of memorial jewelry in the Middle Ages, and took the form of a ring decorated with a skull or a gold skeleton, or a monogram of the dead person with the date of his death worked in hair over the background, which usually was gold. It was customary in wills to leave provision for mourning jewelry. The Puritans were very much against the wearing of jewelry, denouncing plain wedding rings as baubles; the death rings were the only form of jewelry to which they did not object. Toward 1770, a new design in mourning rings, in keeping with the sentimentality of

Mourning clothing, from Harper's Bazar, 1888.

Mourning hats and clothing, from Harper's Bazar, 1888.

the times, made its appearance. The band was of plain gold; the bezel was lozenge-shaped, set with a crystal covering plaited hair and the initials of the dead. These rings often were inscribed with such tender little mottos as—

Prepared Be To Follow Me

or

Death Parts United Hearts

Other rings enclosed a miniature painted in black and sepia upon ivory, depicting a weeping figure standing beside an urn or funeral monument, overshadowed by a willow tree. Hair jewelry came into fashion as mourning jewelry, but was almost entirely confined to English-speaking countries. By the mid-fifties, however, it became fashionable for other than mourning purposes. With the death of Prince Albert in 1881, Queen Victoria ordered that all court jewelry be in dull black, and selected true jet as the official court mourning jewelry. Even before Albert's death, the Queen had been addicted to mourning; in 1850, when mourning the death of the Duke of Clarence, Victoria attended banquets in a black silk dress, wearing jet jewelry. When her mother died, she selected handkerchiefs with black borders. For Albert's death, the width of the black border increased to one inch. Why Victoria chose true jet as the official jewelry is somewhat of a mystery. Certainly one reason would have been the Queen's loyalty to products of her own country. Perhaps it was because the royal couple's first country home at Osborn contained two chairs sewn out of solid blocks of coal, which Albert seemed to like.

Victoria's choice of jet jewelry was reflected inevitably in the type of jewelry selected by American women for their mourning costumes.

The rigid rules of mourning, both in dress and custom, continued to be followed into the '70s. The following is quoted from the editorial pages of the November 8, 1879 issue of *Harper's Bazar*, which gives a clear outline of the state of the art:

"In the South-sea Islands, the gentle heathen wear mourning robes of black and white, striped to denote a mingled sorrow and hope. In Ethiopia, a grayish-brown is chosen, as symbolic of the earth to which the dust returns. Persia decrees pale brown, the color of withered leaves. In Syria, Cappadocia, Armenia and Turkey, sky blue expressed the assured hope that the departed have returned to the skies. The Romans of the Republic wore mourning of dark blue, the emblem of their sober cheerfullness. In China, the choice of white signifies the cherishing of 'white handed hope'. In Egypt and in Burmah, yellow, the hue of the falling leaf, is thought the fittest symbol of death, conveying also, as it does, the hint of exaltation. Only Europe and their own country surround their dead with the emblems of a comfortless despair, and shroud the living in an impenetrable hopelessness of black. Why should it not be that a bit of black ribbon may be made to indicate our bereavement as well as the suffocating crape and serge in which we wrap ourselves? A scarf of black upon the bell pull tells the tale of a loss to passers-by, and no man need to cover his whole house front with funereal drapery.

MOURNING ATTIRE

Widows wear the deepest mourning that is worn, and their veils are longer and the hem deeper. Those who are very conventional as regards mourning do not even have crape on their gowns for some weeks; others again have the entire gown made of crape, jacket and skirt absolutely unrelieved. The first evening gown that a woman wears when she goes out into society after she has been in mourning is generally of crape. Some most effective dinner gowns have been made of crape heavily trimmed with dull jet. All crape walking gowns made with coat and skirt are also trimmed with this dull jet. With such a gown as this a bonnet without a veil is correct, and it can be trimmed with the same style of dull jet, however, not entirely of jet. After six months of deep mourning, some women wear white altogether in the house, trimmed with black ribbons; all put white collars and cuffs on black gowns—the very sheerest linen.

Mourning clothing, from Harper's Bazar, 1898.

"Our present mourning dress is costly, uncomfortable, and in our climate, unwholesome. The fact that the rich wear it imposes it upon the poor, who cannot afford it, and adds to their grief the harassing fear of debt or a new necessity of pinching.

"But there is at least one habit of censure, and that is the ghastly anomaly of wearing these garments as if they were festal raiment. If weeds mean anything, they mean a grief so deep, an experience so absorbing, as to shut out all the usual concerns of life, and encompass the mourning in a solitude of desolation, of which the gloomy garb and the shrouding veil are the adequate emblems. Good taste must demand, therefore, that first mourning should be made with severest simplicity— plain, inexpensive and inconspicuous. Afterward, as time softens the first agony of separation, and worldly interests again assert themselves, it is fitting that a modification of attire would indicate this change of feeling.

"But mourning is essentially a votive garb, and may never display the caprice, costliness or elaboration which are permissible to other dress. Yet everywhere we see it made in accordance with the mode, loaded with trimmings, from lifeless crape to flashing bugles, arrogant with flounces, paniers, over-skirts and with its cost proclaimed in every inappropriate inch. It is even common to wear diamonds, the ultimate expression of the pomp and splendor of worldly life. If anything can discredit the use of mourning, it will be this mindless frippery, this vulgar parody, which is not less a bitter satire on the living than a strange affront to the dead, since it turns the darkest mystery of existence into a vanity of vanities."

Harsh words, but old habits are hard to break. The Victorians went merrily along their way, keeping up the parade of mourning fashions. Some of the fashion houses carried special lines of mourning goods, and the periodicals continued to keep the "dear ladies" informed of the proper mourning etiquette.

The Personal Column of *Harper's Bazar*, November 5, 1881, carried a small item that is indicative of the lengths to which mourning was worn:

"When the Countess Giulia Macchi, the sister of the Pope's maitre de chambre, recently took the veil, the toilettes of the guests were extremely elaborate, in mourning and half mourning styles. One elderly lady wore silver gray satin without trimmings, falling in uninterrupted folds into the long train, with fichu of old point de Bruges, and silver-gray ostrich tips, and lappets of the same lace; a young girl wore lilac Surah, the skirt in vertical puffs separated by rows of large amethyst beads; a lace cape covered the waist, and the throat trimming was a crepe lisse ruche under a dog collar of similar beads."

During the gay '90s, when the craze for jet passementerie reached its peak, Henrietta cloth and crape still were used for dresses trimmed with Kursheedt's Standard Mourning Passementerie composed of dead-jet beads and crape cabachons.

The mourning fashions were carried into the early 1900s, with crape still in use, particularly for the veils. The feeling of protection given by the veil was the reason for its adoption, since it hid the face completely. One of the disadvantages of crape, however, was its weight, and silk veils were available for those who preferred them. Black serge was used for clothing, with the inevitable crape as trimming.

But new ideas were beginning to emerge: "Our excessive summer heat, as well as the delicate health of many women, often make it necessary to follow common sense rather than the conventional rules, and in many cases, the veil must be discarded." By 1909, materials had changed to chiffons, voiles and cashmere; hats were of lighter-weight materials and, although veils were still worn, the length was left to the discretion of the wearer. And the rigid rules were changing too—the length of time for mourning was shortened, as well as the number of people for whom mourning must be worn.

The terrible casualties of World War I and the depression of the 1930s brought additional changes in the mourning rituals. World War II saw the gold star hanging quietly in thousands of windows in homes across the land, the silent sentinal of a shared grief. In the 1970s, quiet memorial services are conducted in small chapels; those in attendance wear their normal, everyday dress. Occasionally, an arm band may be seen. Out of the oppressive rigid rules of Victoriana has come a new attitude and a new concept of death and dying.

CUSTOMS AND CRUSADES

11

Sarah Hale

The Brothers*

That our sons may be as plants grown up in their youth.
—Psalms

As plants, that claim a parent root,
  Are formed and strengthened by each other;
So human minds bear richer fruit
  When brother leans on brother;
Life's purest joys must come unbought
The pearls of love, the gems of thought
The soul's best earthly treasure shines
Uncounted, in our household mines.

And thine has been that happy part
  The prop and guide of one depending;
A precious plant by culture's art
  In holy fruitage ending;
Like palms, whose clasping arms arise
And bear their offerings toward the skies,
Till scarce it seems the plants had birth
In the poor, arid sands of earth.

And was it strange the soul thus taught
  In earth's divinest nurture
Was early to perfection brought
  And reached the heavenward stature;
When Christ in pitying love looks down,
And, by His grace, prepares the crown,
To give his own, their trials o'er,
Celestrial glory evermore!
As latent heat, from earth's control,
  Set free in air is flame ascending;
Thus love, God's image in the soul,
  Is ever upward tending;
But, once sin's flinty barrier broke
It springs, like lightning from the stroke,
And seeks, with fervent zeal, its bliss,
Found only where the Saviour is.

Faith feels all this—and yet their home
  Seems to his sorrowing sisters saddened,
The form beloved can never come
  The voice, the smile that gladdened
Are gone; and oh, the hopes that fall
When one, who was the hope of all,
Their dearest joy and tenderest care,
Hath passed beyond their love and prayer!

THE LATE MRS. SARAH JOSEPHA HALE, AT THE AGE OF EIGHTY-TWO.

Sarah Hale, from Harper's Bazar, 1879.

As when the moon's disk hides the sun,
  Its lustrous noon-day beams concealing;
Look up! the black eclipse is gone,
  A glorious light revealing!
Thus Faith—a moment dark—will rise,
Above the sun, above the skies;
Till in the wondrous vision given,
It sees the precious "plants grown up" in heaven!

Sarah Josepha Hale

Inscribed to Francis De Haes Janvier, on the death of his only brother, Albert Wilson Janvier.

Godey's Lady's Book—1864

Sarah Hale

Sarah Josepha Hale was a paradigm of Victorian virtue. She was devout, highly intelligent, fervently patriotic and the "perfect lady." During her long, rich life, she helped usher in a new era in American history: The causes she espoused with courage and compassion promised a better lot for all mankind—for women as well as men, for the laborers as well as the aristocratic upper class. The following profile of her life is evidence of the mark she made on American customs and attitudes.

Excerpts from the eulogy to Mrs. Sarah Josepha Hale, published June 28, 1879 by *Harper's Bazar*:

This excellent portrait of the pioneer woman-editor of America, who recently died at Philadelphia at the advanced age of ninety-one, possesses an interest both general and historic. Like her contemporary, Madame Patterson Bonaparte, Mrs. Hale's life more than spanned the organized existence of our republic. Born at Newport, New Hampshire, October 24, 1788, she was already a well grown babe when Washington was inaugurated the first President of the United States, and thenceforward she saw the long line of the nation's rulers appear and disappear in succession, until her eyes closed on earthly things during the time of our own President Hayes. It seems like dreaming to recapitulate the events which have been actually seen by one whom we ourselves have known, and who has but this moment passed away from us: it is like hobnobbing with the last century. Washington, Hamilton, Jefferson, Adams and Franklin were as familiar to her childhood as are Grant and Sherman to the boys of today; she was already grown up when the war of 1812 broke out, and was middle-aged at the time of the Mexican war; she beheld the various parties that have striven for power—Federalists and Anti-Federalists, Whigs, Locofocos,

etc.—rise and fall one after another; Jackson, Webster, Clay, Calhoun and like personages were but boys to her as they flitted across the stage; she witnessed the beginning, progress, and the end of the great struggle between freedom and slavery that played so important a part in the history of the nation; and moreover, she saw cities spring up from villages, populous States reclaimed from the wilderness, and the entire West, with the Pacific coast, brought within the pale of civilization. Then, too, what changes were not wrought during her lifetime in literature, such as are admirably summed up as follows by the Boston Traveller: "She was born only thirteen months after Fenimore Cooper, and she survived him almost twenty-eight years; and she published *Northwood* in 1827, the same year in which Cooper published *The Red Rover*, one of the very best of his sea novels, the novelist's reputation then being in the zenith. When *Northwood* was published, Hawthorne was but a youth and had written nothing, and Hawthorne has been sleeping at Concord for fifteen years. Longfellow was still younger, and Holmes was younger than Longfellow, and both are now old men, with reputations as wide as the world. Whittier came upon the stage after she had become known, and Emerson was not very far from the same time."

Mrs. Hale's native place was a charming little New Hampshire town, in the vicinity of the Connecticut River Valley. Her father, Captain Gordon Buell, held a commission under General Gates, and served through the campaign against Burgoyne. He married Miss Martha Whittlesey of Saybrook, Connecticut, a lady of much native energy and highly accomplished for the time. Mrs. Hale was accustomed to ascribe all that she had herself been able to accomplish to her mother's influence. Under her guidance, she pursued her studies and before attaining the age of sixteen had read the works of many of the best English authors. She had also the benefit of the assistance of her elder brother, afterward known as Judge Horatio Buell, of Glen Falls, New York, whose son, James Buell, was president of the Importers' and Traders' Bank of New York City.

In 1830, Mrs. Hale wrote and published a book of poems entitled *Poems for our Children*, which contained several pieces intended to inculcate kindness to the lower animals. One of these, known as "Mary's Lamb" has proved, perhaps, the most popular poem ever composed for children. Wherever the English language is taught, it is a favorite in schoolrooms, and has been the source of quotations, allusions and parodies without number.

Mrs. Hale did not confine her efforts for good objects to her literary labors. Soon after she moved to Boston her attention was drawn to the neglected condition of the seamen belonging to that port, and more especially to their families. Principally by her exertions an association of ladies was organized, under the name of the "Seaman's Aid Society," for the benefit of this class. While she remained in that city, she held the presidency of the society, which did much to remedy the evils it was designed to redress by establishing "Sailor's Homes" and procuring improvements in the laws relating to seamen. An object of a different character, which appealed strongly to her patriotic feelings, presented itself in the unfinished Bunker Hill Monument. Under her leadership, the necessary money to complete the project was earned mainly through a ladies' fair, on a scale much larger than had before been attempted in this country.

A still more important exertion of her power to influence others to good ends was that by which she finally secured the establishment of the time honored New England festival of Thanksgiving Day as a public holiday for the entire nation. For thirty years she had urged, in her various publications, the adoption of the last Thursday in November as the most suitable day for this purpose. By personal correspondence, at first with the Governors of all States, before the Civil War, and afterward with President Lincoln, she at length accomplished this favorite object, which she justly regarded as one of the great works of her life.

The general subject of improving the means of education for women was one to which she devoted great attention. Some of the best known among the institutions which have been recently founded for this object owed either their origin or their plan directly to her suggestions. The founder of Vassar College, the venerable Matthew Vassar, was her attached friend, and consulted her from the inception to the conclusion of his work. It would occupy too much space to enumerate all the useful projects to which she gave the assistance of her pen and her personal influence during the long period of fifty years over which her editorial term extended. Her religious feelings were deep and strong, and her patriotism, kindled by intercourse in childhood with the soliders of the Revolution, was intensely earnest. She had a wide circle of friends, and until her failing sight interrupted it, an extensive correspondence, through which she was able, nearly to the last, to exert an influence in favor of the objects which she had at heart.

As she approached her ninetieth year, the vigor of mind and body which had sustained her through her long and laborious life began to fail. A few months of almost painless illness followed, which closed the 30th of April, 1879, with a death so peaceful that the moment when she ceased to breathe was not perceived by the friends who watched around her.

Excerpts from Sarah's Editor's Table, *Godey's Lady's Book*, 1864:

Life has no resting place on earth. Each stage of our progress is the time of preparation for a new task. No sentence of Holy Writ is more sure and significant than our Saviour's declaration that "for them to whom much is given, of them shall much be required."

These truths should be deeply considered, because great changes are not only coming on the world, but are even now upon us. We allude, particularly, to the new and enlarged opportunities of education, and new advantages of using their powers of mind which are opening for our American women, and that must test not only their own abilities and character, but also influence, in a great degree, the destiny of the nation.

In preparing the Lady's Book, we aim to do good by promoting innocent enjoyment and cheerful improvement. Both of these objects, we think, belong to the economy of God's providence in this world, therefore should be studied and practised in our daily life. Our Heavenly Father made the earth to blossom with beauty and fruitfulness; the air to be pure with life and sweet with fragrance; the birds in bright plumage to sing their songs of joy; the streams to murmur their soft cadences of delight in motion; while the great deep sounds the solemn, yet cheering anthem of perpetual strength in duty, as it ebbs and flows in constant obecience to the laws of God. And all God's laws for our world were intended to promote human happiness in accordance with goodness.

This, then, is our aim: to diffuse and make popular the simple but efficient lessons of home happiness and goodness. Much is in the power of mothers and wives of our land to make happy families, and thus insure a happy nation.

And is not woman—to whom God gave the promise of salvation for our race—next to the angels, the agent of Heaven in preserving goodness?

The Lady's Book has led the way in all the improvements for women which the last thirty years have inaugurated. In the great changes apparently coming on the world there will be a wide scope for the virtue, the affections, and the gifts of womanhood. We shall be careful to watch these coming events and continue to make our Periodical the organ to direct the aspirations and encourage the efforts of WOMAN, always keeping her place in harmony with the Bible prediction of her destiny: "Strength and honor are her clothing, and she shall rejoice in time to come."

—From Volume 68, 1864, Bound Volume of *Godey's Lady's Book* in author's collection.

CUSTOMS AND CRUSADES

12

Mother Jones

Mary Harris Jones was not a fashion-minded woman. While the wealthier women of the Victorian era were thumbing through periodicals, choosing styles, colors and materials for their gowns, "Mother" Jones was standing on a soapbox "agitating." Although she did not have the respect and love of the upper class that Sarah Hale received, Mother Jones, like Sarah, dared to act on her convictions. And act she did, devoting her life to improving the working conditions in American mills and mines, becoming one of the first women in the U.S. to be heard on such a serious subject.

In 1972, *The Autobiography of Mother Jones* was republished by Charles H. Kerr & Company for the Illinois Labor History Society. The book was edited by Mary Field Parton, foreword was written by Clarence Darrow, introduction and bibliography by Fred Thompson. The author expresses her appreciation to the Charles H. Kerr & Company for their permission to use the photograph of Mother Jones' tombstone, and to quote the following from the text of the book.

In 1930, at the age of 100, Mary's strong Irish voice was stilled forever. She was laid to rest in the Union Miner Cemetery, Mount Olive, Illinois. The eulogy by the Reverend Maguire of St. Viator's in Bourbonnais was broadcast over WCFL, the AFL's Chicago station: "Wealthy coal operators and capitalists throughout the United States are breathing sighs of relief while toilworn men and women are weeping tears of bitter grief. Mother Jones is dead." (From the introduction, pages xiii and xiv.)

Mother's Views

In 1880: "Foreign agitators who had suffered under European despots preached various schemes of economic salvation to the workers. The workers asked only for bread and a shortening of the long hours of toil. The agitators gave them visions. The police gave them clubs." (p.17)

In 1903, Mother gathered together a group of children from the mines and mills and marched with them from Pennsylvania to New York to impress upon the conscience of the American people the horror of child slave labor. In every town through which they marched, Mother held meetings:

"A great crowd gathered, professors and students and the people. I told them that the rich robbed these little children of any education of the lowest order that they might send their sons and daughters to places of higher education. That they used the hands and feet of little children that they might buy automobiles for their

108

"Mother" Jones, 1930.
(Charles H. Kerr Publishing Co., see Credits)

On child labor in the mills:

"Little girls and boys, barefooted, walked up and down between the endless rows of spindles, reaching thin little hands into the machinery to repair snapped threads. They crawled under machinery to oil it. They replaced spindles all day long, all day long; night through, night through. Tiny babies of six years old, with faces of sixty did an eight hour shift for ten cents a day. If they fell asleep, cold water was dashed in their faces, and the voice of the manager yelled above the ceaseless racket and whir of the machines. (Page 119)

"Of such is the kingdom of Heaven," said the great teacher. Well, if Heaven is full of undersized, round shouldered, hollow eyed, listless, sleepy little angel children, I want to go to the other place with the bad little boys and girls." (p. 126)

On the West Virginia Coal mines:

"Mining is cruel work. Men are down in utter darkness hours on end. They have no life in the sun. They come up from the silence of the earth utterly wearied. Sleep and work, work and sleep. No time or strength for education, no money for books. No leisure for thought.

With the primitive tools of pick and shovel they gut out the insides of the old earth. Their shoulders are stooped from bending. Their eyes are narrowed to the tiny crevises through which they crawl. Evolution, development is turned backward. Miners become less erect, less wide-eyed.

Like all things that live under ground, away from the sun, they become waxen. Their light is the tiny lamp in their caps. It lights up only work. It lights but a few steps ahead. Their children will follow them down into these strange chambers after they have gone down into the earth forever. Cruel is the life of the miners with the weight of the world upon their backs. And cruel are their strikes. Miners are accustomed to cruelty. They know no other law. They are like primitive men struggling in his ferocious jungle—for himself, for his children, for the race of men." (p. 232, 233)

"Medieval West Virginia! With its ten colonies on the bleak hills! With its grim men and women! When I get to the other side, I shall tell God Almighty about West Virginia!" (p. 235)

wives and police dogs for their daughters to talk French to. I said the mill owners take babies almost from the cradle. And I showed those professors children in our army who could scarcely read or write because they were working ten hours a day in the silk mills of Pennsylvania. The trouble is that no one in Washington cares. I saw our legislators in one hour pass three bills for the relief of the railways but when labor cries for aid for the children they will not listen." (p. 76, 81)

JEWELRY AND TRIMMINGS

13
The Jet Myth

When Queen Victoria chose Whitby Jet as the official mourning jewelry for the royal court in 1861, she hardly realized her action would compound the jet mystique that persists to this day.

True jet has a long history; it was Gagates to the ancients, who named it after the River Gaga or the town of Gagis in Lycia where it was found originally. The modern words Jayet, Jais and Jet are derived from the old name of Gages or Gagat.

> "Lycia her jet in medicine commends;
> But chiefest, that which distant Britain sends;
> Black, light, and polished, to itself it draws
> If warmed by friction near adjacent straws."

Victoria's edict brought a booming business to Whitby, a small village along the Yorkshire coast and the prime source of jet in England. Archaeological evidence dates the use of true jet in ornaments back to the Bronze Age. Whitby originated about 658 A.D. when it became the site of a monastery; Lady Hilda, the grandniece of Edwin, a former king of Northumbria, was its first abbess. Legend has it that the district suffered from a plague of adders around that time. The people of Whitby prevailed upon St. Hilda to use her influence against them. As a result, the snakes' heads were prayed off, and then their bodies were turned into stone.

Little remains of the first abbey save the stone foundation walls; historians doubt whether it was anything more than a building of wood and adobe walls with a thatched roof. Later, the monastery was completely razed by pagan Danes; it was not until the time of William the Conqueror that the abbey was rebuilt (12th Century). For many years the monks at the abbey used crosses and paternostres of true jet; small amounts of true jet jewelry were made in local workshops for sale to the abbey's visitors as souvenirs of their holy pilgrimage.

The first and easiest method of gathering the jet was simply picking up whatever had been washed ashore. The second method was mining; jet miners rented a specified amount of land from its owners and proceeded with their operations. Jet was found in thin laminations, which subsequently thickened to two or three inches in the upper lias strata; a lower bed, from which the best quality was taken, had a thickness of 20 feet and was known as jet rock. Whatever the miners found belonged to them, which they in turn sold to the jet carvers. Should a vein be found that extended beyond the territorial limits of the lease, the miners would have to rent additional land to continue the mining. The third method of obtaining jet was used by a special breed of men known as jet hunters. Using specially anchored ropes, the men would swing out over the cliffs, traversing the face to hunt the veins of jet, while below them the sea crashed at the base of the rocks—no easy task to chip out chunks of jet, transfer them to a sack slung over the shoulder, while being swung about in the ocean winds.

Another site of holy pilgrimages was a town in Spain, Santiago de Compostela (the field of the star). Here the pilgrims were given or sold medals of carved jet as certification of the journey. Although jet workers are known to have been active at Santiago as early as the 10th Century, their craft did not reach its exquisite fulfillment until about the 15th Century. Unfortunately for posterity, the quality of Spanish jet is such that few carvings remain. It is comparatively soft and apt to crack or break up entirely when subjected to sudden heat or cold, due probably to the high percentage of sulphur that most Spanish jet contains.

One of the best descriptions of the state of the jet industry in the 19th Century was written in 1861, "A Glossary of Minerology," by Henry Bristow, published in London:

"Jet is found principally in marly, schistose or sandy beds in France; near Wittemberg in Prussia; in the amber mines on the coast of the Baltic, where it is known by the name of Black Amber; and in Alum shale in the neighbourhood of Whitby in Yorkshire, in hard and dark coloured bituminous shale forming the lower part of the Upper Lias formation. Jet is made into various articles, and is especially used for mourning ornaments. The value of the jet manufactured at Whitby in 1855, amounts to ₤20,000. In France, the department of Aude, of the Var, the Pyrenees, of Ariege, and of Ardennes are celebrated for this production. In the last century 1,200 men were employed in the department of the Aude alone, in carving and turning the jet of that neighbourhood into beads, rosaries, buttons, bracelets, earrings, necklaces, snuff boxes, drinking vessels and into pieces cut in facets, for mourning ornaments. 1000 cwts. were yearly consumed for these purposes, but the trade has now greatly fallen off. Considerable quantities are still, however, exported to Turkey, Senegal, but chiefly to Spain, to which latter country manufactured jet to the value of 18,000 livres were sold in 1805."

By 1884, the search for jet in Whitby had been abandoned and jet from the Pyrenees was sought. The jet hunters were tired of risking life and limb—why go to all that trouble when the jet could be imported so easily? This commerce might have involved French jet imported into Spain, then resold to England, shipped there in long wooden boxes. After the carving and entire ornament were completed, the jet was treated with sealing wax and shellac. The ornaments were then carded, boxed in cotton wool and sold as real Whitby jet. It is not surprising to read it described as having "a velvet, almost waxy, appearance." Sealing wax did the trick.

Jet played a major role in the life of Jean Valjean in Victor Hugo's "Les Miserables." Jean had been sentenced to hard labor for stealing a loaf of bread. After serving his sentence, he was released, finally settling down in the French town of M. sur M., assuming the name of Monsieur Madeleine.

"From time immemorial, M. sur M. had as a special trade the imitation of English jet and German black beads. This trade had hitherto only vegetated, owing to the dearness of the material, which reacted on the artisan . . . Toward the close of 1815, a man, a stranger, had settled in the town, and had the idea of substituting in this trade gum lac for rosin, and in bracelets particularly, clasps of bent metal for welded. This slight change was a revolution; it prodigiously reduced the cost of the material, which, in the first place, allowed the wages to be raised, a benefit for the town; secondly, improved the manufacture, an advantage to the consumer; and thirdly, allowed the goods to be sold cheap, while producing triple the profit, an advantage for the manufacturer.

"In less than three years, the inventor of the process had become rich, which is a good thing, and had made all rich about him, which is better. Thanks to the rapid progress of this trade, which he (Valjean) had so admirably remodeled, M. sur M. had become a place of considerable trade. Spain, which consumes an immense amount of jet, gave large orders for it annually, and in this trade M. sur M. almost rivaled London and Berlin. Father Madelein's profits were so great that after the second year he was able to build a large factory, in which there were two spacious workshops, one for men, the other for women."

Hugo had accumulated notes for 15 years prior to the writing of the novel, and another 15 years in writing it. The characters were built upon people he knew; the description of the way in which Valjean built his fortune also may have been drawn from actual events. The imitation of jet, as well as the export trade to Spain, which built the commerce of M. sur M., are documented in the *Glossary of Minerology*. An interesting side speculation is whether the jet imported to Whitby was jet at all—could it have been a form of imitation as developed by Valjean?

True jet apparently has been the victim of imitation for a long time, even as long ago as the pilgrimages to Santiago de Compostela, when black glass was used for the medals and passed off as the real thing. The *Glossary* has another interesting note: "Artificial jet is

A true jet necklace. The mate to this necklace can be found in "Antique Jewelry and Trinkets," by F.W. Burgess. (Aurora Historical Society, see Credits)

made of a kind of black glass, which is either cut into facets or blown into beads; and the blackness is produced by means of the black wax with which they are filled, or which fastens them to the iron backs on which they are mounted."

When Jenny Lind retired from the operatic stage, she handed her crown to Italian-born, American-raised Adelina Patti, who became known as the great Victorian Prima Donna of Grand Opera. Diminutive of stature, strong willed, with dark expressive eyes and dark hair, Patti possessed many beautiful jewels. Yet she apparently had a fondness for true jet, and had her photograph taken in 1867, wearing a long jet chain and jet ball drop earrings. As so often happens, her particular liking stimulated a demand for jet jewelry among the middle classes, and from this the jet myth began to grow in proportion. Businessmen, always alert to a new opportunity, quickly turned to the more easily obtainable black glass, imitating true jet in a dull finish. The black glass was marketed under the names of French Jet, Cut Jet, Faceted Jet and Imitation Jet. As time went on the single word Jet came to be used, just as today many consumer products are known in general by one brand name.

Black glass actually was called jet long before this happened, and probably acquired the name because of the color. Black beads are found in much of the old beadwork tapestries and laces of the 16th and 17th Centuries. In 1723, Savary wrote in his *Dictionnaire Universel du Commerce:* "It is with artificial jet, cut and pierced and threaded with silk or thread, that embroideries are made in sufficient good taste, but very

dear, which are used, particularly in churches. Trimmings are also made of it in half mourning for men and women, and sometimes muffs and tippets, and trimmings for robes."

In Murano in 1790, Georgio Barbaria requested a patent for making black bottles for export to England, also enamels and jet.

While Worth's introduction of jet passementerie in 1855 got off to a slow start, Victoria's choice of true jet for court mourning jewelry, coupled with the Civil War in the United States, propelled "jet" into the fashion language of the day. As war casualties mounted, jet beadwork, with matching jet jewelry, was seen everywhere on the costumes of the day. Fashion columns in periodicals included detailed descriptions of the proper mourning dress for both day and evening wear, and the correct jewelry to be worn with each costume, usually jet.

The workshops of Whitby were small and a great deal of the work was hand carving. The total output could not have supplied the British and American demand for true jet jewelry. The toy makers of Birmingham, England, who had been making jewelry for a long time, were an obvious source of craftsmen for jet, made in the dull finish at first, as time went on the black glass appeared as we know it today—shiny and faceted.

As the use of jet (black glass) passementerie on clothing increased in the 1870s, "the demand for jet jewelry mounts to a fureur. The Whitby jet and the brilliant faceted variety—known as black garnet—enjoy equal favor"; continuing into the 1880s and 1890s, the single word jet was used more and more. Translating the old fashion columns into modern day speech, two questions usually come to mind: Is the jet jewelry so frequently mentioned true jet, black glass, or another material made to imitate jet, as M. sur M. had done so successfully? From whence did the river of black glass originate?

Although glass was manufactured in America, the earliest glass houses generally were small, popped up here and there, and disappeared almost as quickly. It was not until 1893, when the Libbey Glass Co. in Ohio was established, that the glass industry found its permanent home. The American glass houses of the 19th Century concentrated their efforts on producing bottles, flasks, tableware, window glass, lamp glass, chemical apparatus, druggist wares and articles of daily use. New Jersey was an early glass making center, and its proximity to New York and Philadelphia—early jewelry making centers helped the glass makers sell jet to the jewelry firms—who in turn assembled the pieces into finished ornaments.

The history of it points especially to a small country known as Bohemia prior to World War I, today known as Czechoslovakia. Glass has been traced back to the 13th Century in this country, where it usually served the needs of the church and the Bohemian nobility. By the end of the 14th Century, glass was being exported to neighboring countries. The early Bohemian crystal glass was of high quality, and as early as the 1680s, was exported to England and Europe. The glassworkers of Silesia (until 1742 a part of Bohemia) developed a high degree of artistic skill and technical efficiency, excelling in the engraving of glass.

By 1730, trading posts had been established in 50 principal cities of Europe and Mexico, as well as in Baltimore and New York. Inspired by the success of Wedgewood's "Black Basaltes" ware, in 1822 a new glass called "Hyalith" was introduced by the Bohemians. Jet black and fired with gold chinoiserie, Hyalith was used for coffee table ware, for making perfume bottles, bowls and bases. This was followed by the famous "Ruby" glass and other colored glasses—cobalt, turquoise, chrysophrase, uranium—with fired-gold or enamel-painted decorations. The Bohemians developed the Chinese technique of overlay glass, which is a core of crystal glass with one or more layers of transparent or opaque glass. Modern production methods of glassmaking during the second half of the 19th Century simplified and quickened the process of glass manufacture, and cheap, machine-made, pressed glassware was produced.

When Vienna emerged as a fashion center during the Franco-Prussian War, Austrian businessmen were quick to take advantage of the situation. After Bohemia was swallowed by Austria, the Austrians made certain the glasshouses stayed in Bohemia, close enough to watch and control, but far away enough to prevent smoke and soot from soiling the sparkling Viennese cities. The fantastic business opportunity opened up by the fortunes of war was quickly seized. Since clothing was exported, what better time to push additional exports of glassware, beads and beadwork and buttons!

By the late 1870s, the ready-to-wear garment industry was shifting into high gear in the United States, while the home sewing machines were whizzing along guided by the nimble fingers of the "do it yourselfers." By the 1880s the "jet craze" was going into an upswing and imports were needed to keep up with the demand. Tables showing the imports of glass into the U.S. between 1876 and 1880 gave "Bohemia, cut, engraved, painted, coloured, printed, stained, silvered, gilded, plain, molded and pressed" glass a value of $2,972,089.00. These imports must have brought the black glass beads for necklaces and passementerie beadwork; the shapes for insertion into brooches, earrings and bracelets; and, conceivably, some of the completed pieces of jewelry and hat ornaments were made entirely in Bohemia.

World War I left its mark on old Bohemia. Published in 1930, authoress Dorothy Giles, in her book *The Road Through Czechoslovakia*, made particular note of the cheap jewelry, cheap glass and cheap beads, beads, beads, found everywhere in Prague. After World War II, the Czechs meticulously rebuilt their glass industries; most notably, they led in the development of fine rhinestones for jewelry. By the 1950s, Paris jewelers who specialized in making jewelry exclusively for the couture trade used the imitation Czech gems because of their precise calibration. Paris beadwork houses imported Czech beads by the bag in every color of the rainbow.

The final chapter of the Whitby jet story was written during World War I, which brought a brief flurry of activity in jewelry making. Many believed that the earlier substitution of Spanish jet had contributed to the downfall of Whitby, with the competition from black glass finishing the job. Now with both glass and Spanish jet supplies cut off, jet mining was started again and black ornaments were made for mourning use. But most of the workers had grown old and the young men were off to the service of their country. Hope was held that after the war's conclusion and the return of the younger men, the old Whitby jet industry would revive. These hopes were never realized. The old abbey, ravaged now by time and the buffeting of the ocean winds, suffered one of its final blows in 1914 when a German cruiser bombarded the Yorkshire coast. Whitby and its wondrous jet now are entered into the rolls of the antiquities, leaving the jet myth to posterity.

JEWELRY AND TRIMMINGS

14

The Glory of Glass

Glass is so much a part of our daily lives that we scarcely give it a second thought or consider its long history. All too often a lovely piece of costume jewelry is discarded simply because it is set with "cheap glass." Such low regard for glass was not the rule 5,000 years ago.

In 1922, after five weary years of searching for one particular tomb, the sun god Re finally led the way to the steps, concealed for centuries by rubble and debris. When the tomb finally was opened, the imagination of the world was shaken, and the name of King Tut became a household word. Here was a magnificent archaeological find—for the first time the burial customs for a Pharoah—a Pharoah dead nearly 33 centuries—were revealed, intact. Among the treasures was an artifact that surpassed all others—a funerary mask wrought in solid gold, beaten and burnished—the stripes of the headdress set with blue glass, the eyes of quartz and obsidian (natural black glass), and the eyelids and eyebrows picked out in lapis lazuli. During the Middle Kingdom (2154-1570 B.C.), goldwork frequently was inlaid with glass pastes, forming necklaces, bracelets, anklets, belts, rings and earrings. From the tomb of Thutmose III (1501-1447 B.C.) came a stunning gold collar containing carnelian, green feldspar and glass.

The Phoenicians learned the art of glassmaking from the Egyptians, and the Greeks in turn learned from the Phoenicians. In the Golden Age of Greece—450 B.C.—a massive statue of Zeus of Olympia was constructed. Forty feet high, the statue was composed mainly of gold and ivory. Materials used for small detail were ebony, precious stones, glass and obsidian. A small gold shrine with Dionysus and a satyr in the National Museum of Athens is set with semi-precious stones, especially garnets, and cornelian, sardonyx and glass paste.

After Greece fell to the Romans, the captured Greek goldsmiths were put to work making jewelry for Imperial Rome. According to Pliny, Roman glass factories were kept busy constantly turning out bangles and beads. Nor were Roman husbands any different from modern-day men in grumbling about their wives' spending: "Hey!" said Habinnas, "You cleaned me out to buy you a glass bean. Honestly, if I had a daughter, I'd cut her little ears off. If there weren't any women, everything would be dirt cheap."

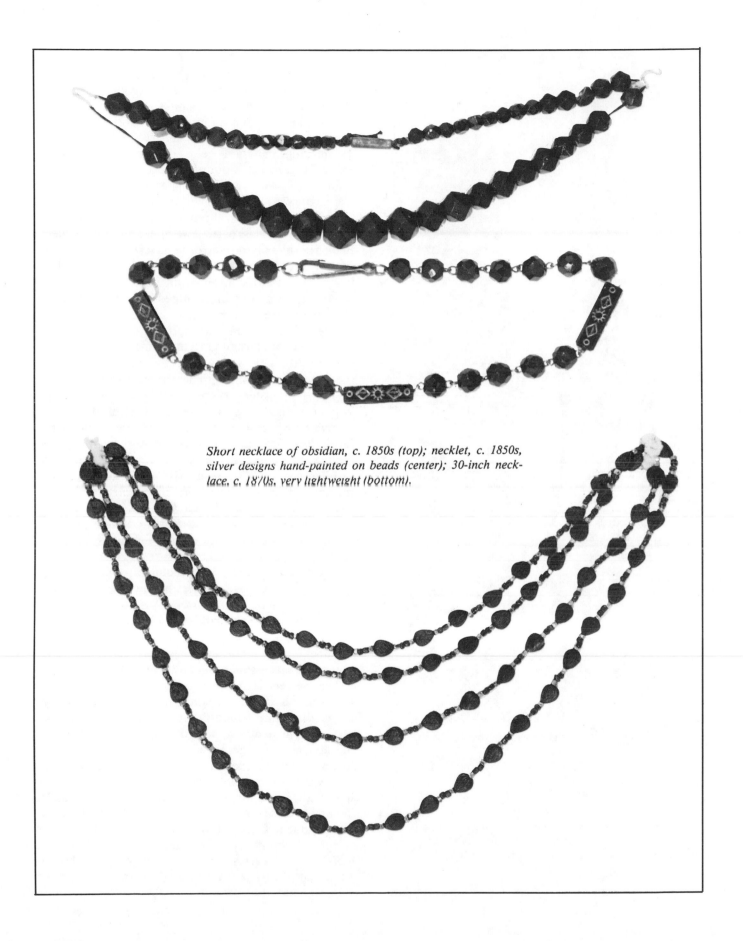

Short necklace of obsidian, c. 1850s (top); necklet, c. 1850s, silver designs hand-painted on beads (center); 30-inch necklace, c. 1870s, very lightweight (bottom).

Jet necklaces: 54 inches long, unusually shaped beads, c. 1880s (left); 44 inches long, unusually shaped beads, in white, black and blue-gray, spaced with silver beads, c. 1880s (right).

During the dark ages, the secret of glass was saved by the monks. As the power of the church grew during the 11th Century, the artisan monks used their skills in glassmaking and goldsmithing to the glory of God. Alchemists of the 14th Century left recipes behind them for making imitation gems of glass—false rubies, emeralds, garnets, turquoise. By the 15th Century, the stained glass windows of European cathedrals glowed like rare jewels.

In the Victorian era, those who could not afford real diamonds wore glass paste jewelry in imitation of them. French paste is often referred to as strass jewelry—after Joseph Strasser, a Viennese glass maker who lived in Paris and, in 1810, invented an improved method of faceting glass and adding colored foils beneath tinted glass to increase its intensity.

It remained for Louis Comfort Tiffany (1845-1933) to create the most glorious glass of all for America. Son of the founder of the famous Tiffany store, Louis chose the career of artist and designer rather than following in his father's footsteps. He became interested in glass and began experimenting endlessly. He first produced decorative glass tiles used for fireplaces and lighting fixtures. His first stained-glass windows were created around 1885, and in 1894 came Favrile glass, irridescent and lustrous. Of all the glass Tiffany created, perhaps the most illustrious was the drop curtain for the National Theater in Mexico City—200 panels, each three feet square, containing nearly a million pieces of glass. When assembled, the curtain weighed a total of 27 tons; operated by hydraulic pressure and counter balances, only seven seconds were required to raise or lower the screen. Louis was forgotten by the time of his death in 1933, and much of his work was consigned to the trash heap as utterly worthless. Today, the contribution he made to the world of glass has been recognized; genuine Tiffany lamps and glassware command fabulous prices that would probably astonish their creator.

The theaters of America became another showplace for wondrous displays of glass, particularly in the stage costumes. Sarah Bernhardt's professional clothes were one example, and have been described as works of art. She designed all of her theatrical wardrobe with meticulous attention to detail, and her usual disregard for cost. Silks were woven to her order in Lyon, her velvets were imported from Italy and her furs came from Russia. Trimming and embroidery were splashed on with reckless abandon. One costume created especially for her role of Theodora in 1884-1885 contained more than 4,500 "gems," each sewn on by hand. When the beautiful Lillian Russell was introduced by Tony Pastor, she stepped onto the stage in a white voile dress, shot

20th Century black glass: c. 1920s with metal setting (top); c. 1950s—dog collar choker style (bottom).

The Imitator: choker in early plastic, c. 1920s .

through with bugle beads, which shimmered and glistened under the gaslights. Later, when she added her collection of little doo-dads from Diamond Jim to her stage dress, the audience must have been half blinded by the flashing reflections as Lillian moved on stage!

Glass was often a visitor to the White House inaugural balls. The First Ladies often chose ball gowns rich with beadwork for the event. Caroline Scott Harrison (1889-1892) chose a silver gray faile, with the collar and trimmings of the waist in gold and silver beads. Mary McKee, daughter of President Harrison, wore a satin brocade gown with the V-shaped neck opening hung with a network of amber and silver beads. Helen Herron Taft (1909-1913) had her white silk chiffon sent to Tokyo for embroidery in silver thread and crystal beads.

Glass has come a long way since it was first set into King Tut's mask. Of all the forms we know in glass jewelry, beads are probably the Adam and Eve of the family. Indeed, beads literally have rolled themselves around the world. In every culture, at some time, there were beads, beads, beads. The Egyptian word for bead was sha-sha, and the syllable sha was the word for luck. In English, bead comes from the old Anglo-Saxon word bede, meaning a prayer. As prayers were repeated they had to be counted in some way—and in the course of time the word was transferred from the prayers themselves to the knots or beads on which they were counted.

Bead making of the past primarily has been associated with Venice, and in particular, Murano. As the secret of glass making began to spread across Europe, new centers of trading were developed. As early as 1549, glasshouses were set up in England. Between 1608 and 1680, a large glass industry flourished in Amsterdam, which probably supplied the Dutch East India Company with trade beads. By the 16th Century, the first bead furnaces were set up in Bohemia; by the 17th Century, beads were produced in Germany, Holland, Italy and Venice. England imported vast quantities of beads from the Continent, and in turn exported them to Africa, the English Colonies and the West Indies. Repeal of the glass tax in England meant that the beads could be made in English glassworks instead of being imported. Amber, rose, turquoise blue and green are the earlier colors used in England, while crimson, dark greens and grays date to 1880.

Bib necklaces of latticed jet, or triple rows of faceted jet beads were high fashion for mourning in 1837. The fashion then changed and the early Victorian necklaces can more correctly be described as necklets, for they were nearly all of shorter length than the necklace, coming just below the base of the throat, being a little longer in front than the choker necklace. Gradually, the length of the string was increased, influenced, no doubt,

20th Century black glass.

Top to bottom: contemporary lucite bracelet; contemporary adaptation of coiled wire bead bracelet; black glass shapes strung on elastic, similar to the shapes used in true jet bracelets—c. 1870s.

Top to bottom: five-strand wire bracelet with intermixed dull and bright jet beads of odd shapes; contemporary bracelet in heavy metal setting, hinge on each side of center medallion; The Vester patented bracelet. At one time there probably was a pearl in the center of the medallion.

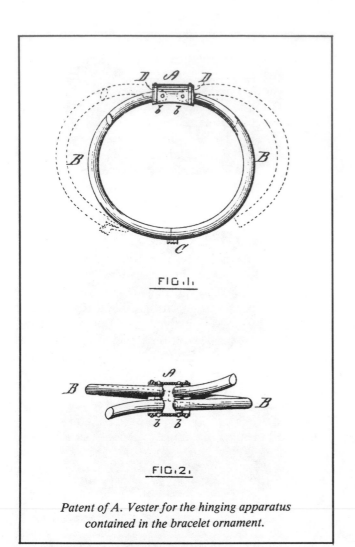

FIG. 1.

FIG. 2.

Patent of A. Vester for the hinging apparatus contained in the bracelet ornament.

Jet brooch: purchased from the Art Institute of Chicago, Ill. dated 1860 with painted metal back. Facets may have been fastened to the back by means of wax.

by the long fine chains that the Victorian ladies held in such high esteem. In the 1870s, the Benoiton chain hung from the bonnet to the waist. In the eighties and nineties, long jet necklaces still were worn, but the dog collar was high fashion. For the wealthy, pearls and diamonds were used for the collar that fit closely to the throat, and were as much as two inches deep, fit with gold bar stiffeners and a stiff clasp to make sure they stood up all around the base of the neck. From these evolved the less expensive jet collars. The revival of jet during World War I and later in the 20s brought both the long and short necklaces. A *Sears Roebuck Catalogue* of the 20s featured: "Imported imitation jet beads—30" long—$1.25 ea." The catalogue illustration gives every indication these are the typical black glass faceted beads, graduated in size. By 1926, the cubist movement influenced jewelry design; the dresses eventually went to knee length and choker strands of beads were worn that were as large as ping pong balls.

The true jet bracelets of early Victoriana generally were large, chunky shapes strung on narrow elastic; the shapes might be round, square, oval, octagonal, with the edges slightly bevelled. Such shapes were a natural since they brought out the qualities of the material. The serpentine bracelet was another design, as well as the Etruscan; carved jet medallions were fastened to other materials—brass, celluloid, etc., which formed the wristband.

As black glass took over, the same large chunky shapes were used for bracelets strung on elastic. However, their size gradually diminished. Beads also were strung on heavy wire, from a single strand to multiple strands. The 1895 Christmas edition of the *Peoples Home Journal* offered as a premium: "Ladies Cut Jet Bracelets, 38 separate cut jet balls (beads) on a single heavy strand of wire, which curls about the wrist."

A description of a very glamorous jet bracelet appeared in a 1920 issue of the *Woman's Home Companion:* "Novelties noted during race week include slender jet bracelets, inset with ivory figures, such as elephants or birds. Other ivory and jet bracelets are thickly encrusted with tiny jewels—emeralds, rubies and diamond dust."

In 1947, among a wealth of jewelry sold at auction was a jet bead bracelet, platinum clasp set with two small round diamonds, bracelet of four strands of jet beads—auction price, $500.00.

Of all the jewelry loved by the Victorian ladies, the favorite was the brooch, or breast pin. After the chains, necklaces, bracelets, earrings, hair combs and tiaras were loaded on, the brooch was added, and the cameo brooch is the one most associated with this era.

Victorian black glass cameos. Upper left: molded in one piece, c. 1860s. Other cameo backs were cut from sheets of glass, with the cameo head applied separately. Lower right cameo has two layers of glass. The sheet glass cameos all have a purple case when held to light.

Cameos

A true cameo has a design produced by cutting away portions of the upper layers of stone or shell, leaving an underlayer as a background. Cameos have been prized since the time of Alexander the Great. The art of cameo carving reached its peak during the early part of the Roman Empire. Agates predominately were used in Greek carving, since the natural color bandings made sharp contrasts possible. In addition to the agates, the Greeks used aquamarina for the engraving of their marine gods, due to its similarity to the color of the sea. They always carved the features of Bacchus in amethyst —the stone that suggested the purple flow of wine.

The Romans became so enamored of the Greek cameo they often strung them together to form an entire necklace. The crusaders liberated bushels of gems from the infidels which they in turn presented to the church on their return to their native lands. Contained in this loot were many cameos representing the Roman and Greek gods, which the clergy used to adorn their shrines and vestments. Just as the Romans had placed other names on the Greek gods when they adopted the gods for their own, now the clergy renamed the pagan gods and goddesses after the figures of Christianity. Venus was called the Virgin Mary; Jupiter was an Archangel and winged Cupids were known as Cherubim. Triptyches of the Virgin were adorned with cameos of the pagans.

The cameo faded for a while only to be revived during Napoleon's Egyptian campaign, by the excavation of Herculaneum and Pompeii. Empress Josephine was so enamored of cameos she persuaded Napolean to loot the royal treasury, taking the cameos and, like the Romans, stringing them together to form a necklace.

In the 18th Century, Josia Wedgewood made cameos in the revered classical style. In 1815 some of the original Parthenon marbles arrived in England; Lord Elgin found them heaped upon the ground and prevailed upon the Turks to allow him to crate the marbles and take them to England, where they have since been named the Elgin marbles. Here in sweeping panorama are the gods and goddesses of ancient Greece—Dionysus, Theseus, Poseidon, Apollo, Demeter, Persephone and Athena. Small wonder that classical Greek heads were so prevalent in Victorian jewelry—here were the originals to use as models. Of all the Greek gods and goddesses, Athena's likeness is the one most frequently found.

The very early glass cameos were treated as gemstones and were carved by hand. The majority were first formed in a mold taken from a gem cameo and finished by a lapidary so that the detail was as fine as the original.

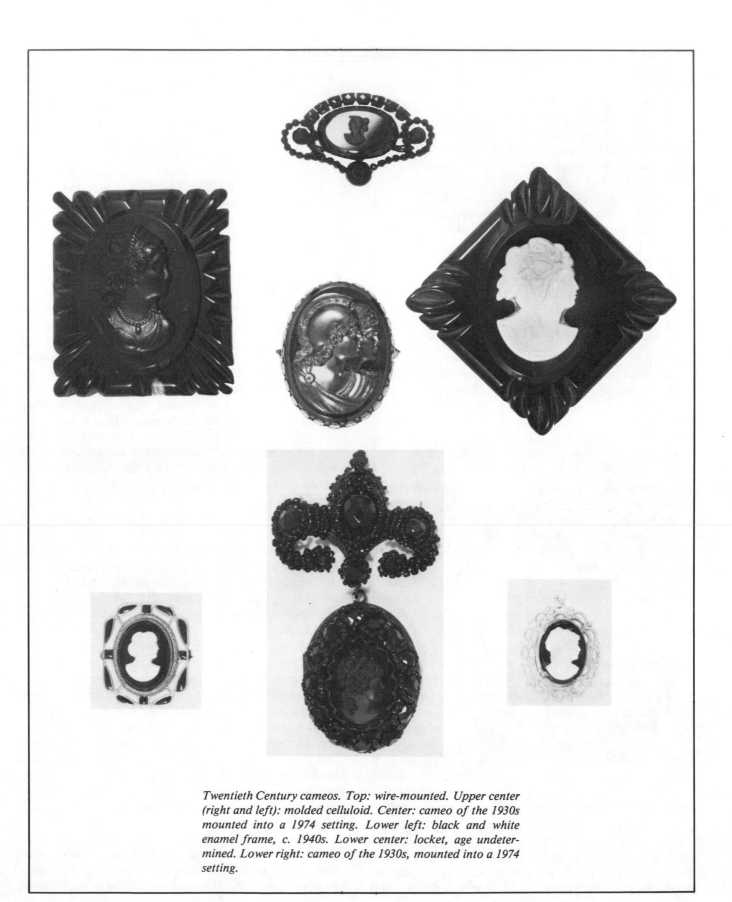

Twentieth Century cameos. Top: wire-mounted. Upper center (right and left): molded celluloid. Center: cameo of the 1930s mounted into a 1974 setting. Lower left: black and white enamel frame, c. 1940s. Lower center: locket, age undetermined. Lower right: cameo of the 1930s, mounted into a 1974 setting.

In making the glass cameo, man-made glass was layered to approximate the bicolored strata of gem stones, other minerals and shells. Such cameos were made as long ago as the classical periods of Greece, Rome and Byzantium.

In the early part of the Victorian era, molded glass cameos were made in large numbers, mounted in brass settings, or used as the centers of buttons. These early cameos usually were large and oval in shape; the lady of the fifties wore them under her chin and right in the center of her high fastened collar. This style of wearing the brooch continued into the Seventies and Eighties when fashion called for high, plain necks and tightly buttoned bodices, and into the '90s, when they were worn at the neck of riding habits.

For evening wear, with low-cut necklines, the brooch became a pendant, or was mounted on a velvet neckband or collarette. With the brooch, a locket and chain would sometimes be worn, but this fashion faded by the 1890s.

As time went on, from the molded glass cameos, the glass then was poured into sheets, with the glass between the designs left thin so the cameo could be cut apart with a simple tool. The tool was made to fit exactly the different size of cameos, and a single turn freed each cameo from the sheets. Thus, the cameos were produced quickly and cheaply, but as usually happens, the quality suffered and the designs did not stand in clear detail. The cameos were backed with tin plate, similar to tin can metal; for the black glass cameo, the tin was painted black. Because of the thinness of the glass, when held to the light, the edges of such black glass cameos frequently have a purple cast, and are called amethyst cameos. This method of cameo production probably was used after 1870.

The cameo brooch began to fade from favor during the Eighties, and finally disappeared by the turn of the century. It was revived in the 1920s, when cameos were set into large frames of celluloid. At this time the glass of the cameos was much thicker, with a more precise appearance. By the 1930s, no one would be caught dead wearing a cameo—they were for the little gray-haired old ladies. In the 1970s, the old cameos are being dragged out of hiding and worn with great pride—''Why, this belonged to my grandmother!''

One last word about the cameo. According to the definition prepared by the National Better Business Bureau and the American Gem Society some years ago, cameos should be distinguished as stone cameos or shell cameos. If cameos were molded or pressed, they should be described as such; for example, one molded of glass should be called a glass cameo, molded cameo or imitation cameo. But a cameo is a cameo is a cameo, regardless of its origin, just as black glass is still jet.

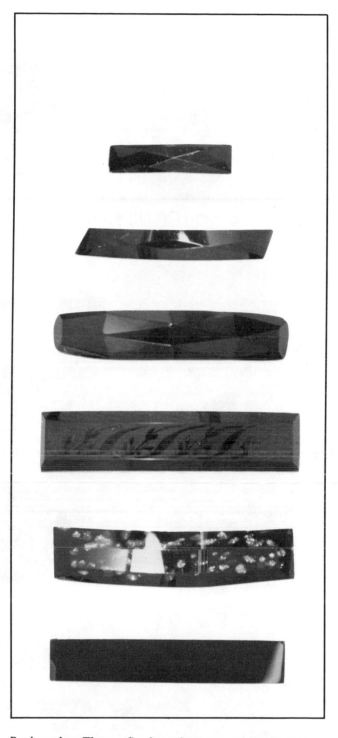

Bar brooches. The top five brooches are curved to fit the base of the throat. Fifth brooch down is of goldstone. All have simple ''C'' clasps. The bottom brooch has safety-pin style clasp, and dates c. 1920s.

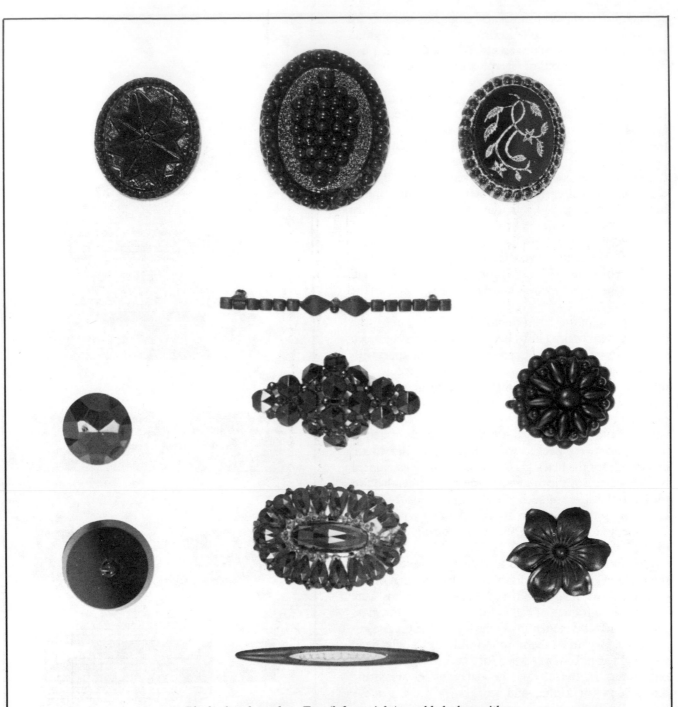

Black glass brooches. Top (left to right): molded glass with simple "C" clasp, c. 1880;s grape cluster design; outlined in silver, hand-applied. Top center: slender wire-mounted dull glass mourning pin, c. 1870s. Middle center: Two brooches set with facets, safety-pin type clasp, turn of the century. Center bottom: Dull black glass set with seed pearls, gold mounting; mourning brooch, turn of the century. Right center: mourning pin of stamped metal, black glass center, c. 1900s.

*20th Century black glass (1950-1975)
with metal settings and safety glass.*

Jet pendant, c. 1970s with gold-colored metal setting.

An issue of the *Scientific American* magazine devoted space to a description of a patent issued by W.O. Draper, A.C. Sweetland and G.H. Draper for cluster work jewelry. In this process, the glass was molded in one piece, the surface raised to form bosses (a type of facet). A latticework metal setting fit over the face of the molded glass, with each boss projecting into a small opening. The finished appearance gave the impression that each facet was set into the metal separately—that old Yankee ingenuity at work again!

The passementerie method of fastening glass to its setting is well known to button collectors. The small, separately molded little facets are fastened by means of small wires at the back of the facet into the perforated metal back. The 1861 *Glossary* described the early method of fastening by means of wax. The wire fasten-

ing method can be dated from the following note in *Demorest's Monthly Magazine*, April, 1886:

"Ornamental pins and slides of cut glass of such as were worn twenty years ago are in fashion. They are much more artistic than the old style, being of fine quality and exquisitely finished, and vary in size from an inch in length to three or four inches. The pins are riveted so they are much more durable than formerly. They have alternate bars or blocks of polished and dull jet. Riveted jet in very fine quality will be in great demand."

The term "riveted" as applied to the jet ornaments no doubt grew from its similarity in appearance to the cut steel faceted jewelry and shoe buckles, where the small steel facets each were individually riveted to the frames.

By 1880, the bar brooch began to appear. Smaller, lighter than the larger shapes of the '60s and '70s, the bar brooches adapted well to mass production, for by this time the industrial revolution was gaining momentum and much of the jewelry was thinner, cheaper and flashier. The bar was made in varying sizes, and in the black glass, usually slightly curved with a faceted edge to fit the contour of the throat.

One of the most interesting of the bar brooches shown is the one termed goldstone. Originally called aventurine, goldstone has the distinction of being one of the few things whose name was borrowed for the later discovery of a natural aventurine. The goldstone process was discovered by chance (par aventure) about 1810 and manufactured for a long period of time at the glassworks in Murano, Italy. A workman accidentally allowed some brass filings to fall into a pot of melted glass, and named it aventurine on the spot.

The golden iridescence of the glass is caused by a crystalline separation of metallic copper from the mass. The molten glass is allowed to cool slowly to facilitate the formation of crystals. Trapped air forms bubbles, which help to show the sparkle of the copper. Lapidarists term goldstone the only man-made stone. During the Victorian era, the natural aventurine was found in Bohemia, France, Spain and Siberia, and fashioned into ring stones, shirt studs, earrings, snuff boxes and other ornamental articles.

It is virtually impossible to date much of the old jet jewelry with accuracy. Styles evolved much more slowly than they do today, and production methods in the 1860s and 1870s were not as efficient as they were by the 90s. One clue in the older brooch is the catch, which usually takes the form of a letter "C" and has no moving parts. A modern safety catch contains a rotating sleeve which closes the gap and secures the pin. The older pin often seems to be quite long, protruding about a quarter of an inch beyond the limit of the brooch. The

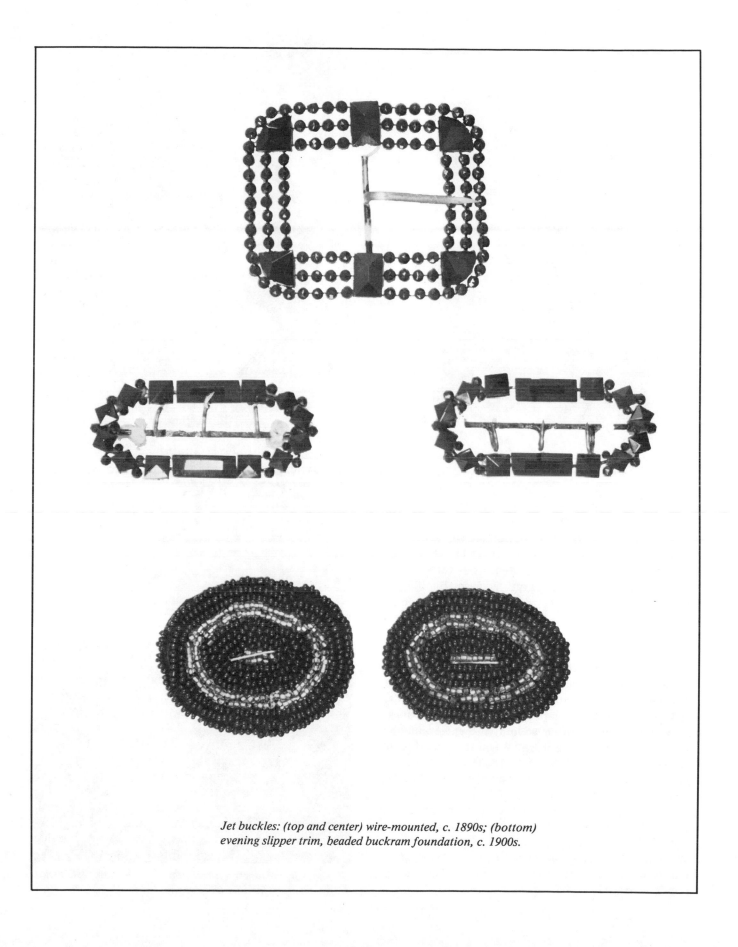

*Jet buckles: (top and center) wire-mounted, c. 1890s; (bottom)
evening slipper trim, beaded buckram foundation, c. 1900s.*

Jet cufflinks: (top) c. 1920s; (center) c. 1880-1890s; (bottom) c. 1950s.

Earrings from Harper's Bazar (top, 1897; bottom, 1880) with drops and in the familiar hoop shape.

extra length was used to catch the pointed end again into the fabric for a little extra security. The breastpin patented by T.W.F. Smitten, September 1, 1868, shows the longer pin and the "C" type of clasp. By 1890, a patent issued to D.F. Adams showed a broader type of hook, with the base of the pin hinge enclosed. The safety pin type of clasp emerged in the mid 1890s.

The fashions in earrings changed several times during the Victorian era. In the Romantic period (1837-1850) long earrings were worn, although the return to ringlets in the mid 1840s nearly obliterated them. By the 1850s, hair styles revealed the ears and small, neat earrings, half moon in shape, often wide at the ends; and the round, hoop shapes were worn. When the Grand Style was ushered in during the early 1860s, drop earrings were back, and often were so long they tangled with bonnet strings. When Charles Worth succeeded in banishing the bonnet, the earrings became an important factor in styling the coiffure; earrings and hair combs often were designed in matching sets for afternoon wear. The Grand Style continued until the 1890s, when small studs were popular, or none at all; by 1897, drop earrings were back.

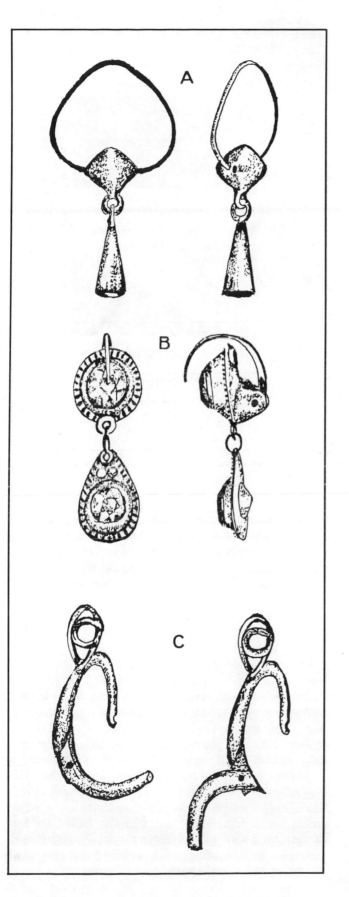

Among the early military outposts in the New World was Fort Michilimackinac, settled by the French about 1715. Located on the Straits of Mackinac, the French retained control until about 1761, when it was taken over by the British, who commanded the fort until 1781. The fort was then torn down and rebuilt on Mackinac Island, a more defensible position.

Since 1959, the old fort has been under continuous archaeological and historical investigation under the auspices of the State of Michigan, Department of Natural resources, Mackinac Island State Park Commission, and the Michigan State University Museum and Department of Anthropology.

Among the thousands of artifacts uncovered were innumerable pieces of jewelry, many with glass jewels in blue, green, red and clear glass; in pewter, brass and silver mountings. Beads of every size, shape and color were found, including the black faceted variety.

The earrings pictured here are from the digs: A is a silver earring showing the slender wire circle which passed through the ear lobe and slipped into the top ball of the earring. B is made of brass, with a colored glass set. The curved, pointed brass ear piece hinges back to allow the point to pass through the ear. C is of gilt brass, also with a hinged section to secure the earring into place.

The author expresses her appreciation to the Mackinac Island State Park Commission for permission to photograph these examples of early earring fasteners, which appear in Fort Michilimackinac 1715-1781 by Lyle M. Stone, published by Michigan State University, East Lansing, Michigan, 1974, an American Revolution Bicentennial Project.

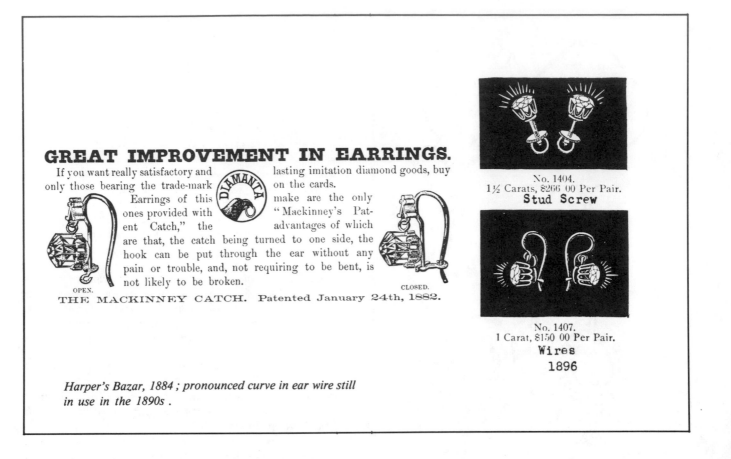

GREAT IMPROVEMENT IN EARRINGS.

If you want really satisfactory and only those bearing the trade-mark ~~DIAMANTA~~ lasting imitation diamond goods, buy on the cards. Earrings of this make are the only ones provided with "Mackinney's Patent Catch," the advantages of which are that, the catch being turned to one side, the hook can be put through the ear without any pain or trouble, and, not requiring to be bent, is not likely to be broken.

OPEN.   CLOSED.

THE MACKINNEY CATCH. Patented January 24th, 1882.

No. 1404.
1½ Carats, $266 00 Per Pair.
Stud Screw

No. 1407.
1 Carat, $150 00 Per Pair.
Wires
1896

Harper's Bazar, 1884 ; pronounced curve in ear wire still in use in the 1890s .

For all this time, ears were pierced, a practice which began centuries before. Specimens of the earrings worn by Egyptian and Greek ladies may be seen in museums. Roman ladies displayed their ostentation principally in their earrings, and there were female dealers in Rome who earned a handsome living by healing the ears of ladies who had torn the lobes by wearing pendants of exaggerated weight. Thus, the Victorian ladies merely were following a time-honored custom in having their ears pierced, even when the practice was described as "a relic of barbarism, which pierces the flesh to introduce ornaments," and "if the ear is beautifully made in it-self, it is an ornament to the human head, which will only be marred by piercing it."

By 1882, the Mackinney Catch was advertised for earrings, and may well have been the earliest form of the safety clasp so common on brooches today. In 1890, the *American Woman* magazine contained the following comment on its fashion pages:

"Earrings, it is said, are once more making their appearance in the upper circles of society. It is there of course, that fashions are set. So in time, they will probably become common. To make these barbaric little ornaments popular, the jewelers are contriving the most sensible little attachments by which earrings can be worn comfortably and no cruel hole forced through the under lobe. From the top of the ring, a thread-like gold hoop passes up into the hollow of the ear in front, and at the back a little gold foot lies under the tender lobe with a firm yet not annoying pressure. Thus the ornament is hung on safely and painlessly."

This probably was the forerunner of the screw-back earring that came into being about 1910-15. In the 1890s the looped wire was caught in a tiny hook below the ear to fasten it more securely, and the stud screw also was worn. This usually was in the form of a diamond with a straight post that passed through the lobe of the ear, onto which a small round disc screwed to the threaded end of the post at the back of the underlobe. Another type of earring catch was patented by H. Sessler in 1890. The spring wire of the loop was caught into a small spring jaw, holding it in place. The tiny ball at the end of the spring wire was "sufficiently small to be passed through the perforation of the ear lobe" and prevented the spring wire from slipping out of the jaw.

B. ALTMAN & CO.—CATALOGUE

No. 22. Black Garnet Ear Rings, 30c.

No. 24. Black Garnet Ear Rings, 50c.

No. 25. Whitby Jet Ear Rings, 65c.

No. 27. Whitby Jet Ear Rings, 65c.

B. Altman & Co. catalogue, 1879-1880. (Harvard University, see Credits)

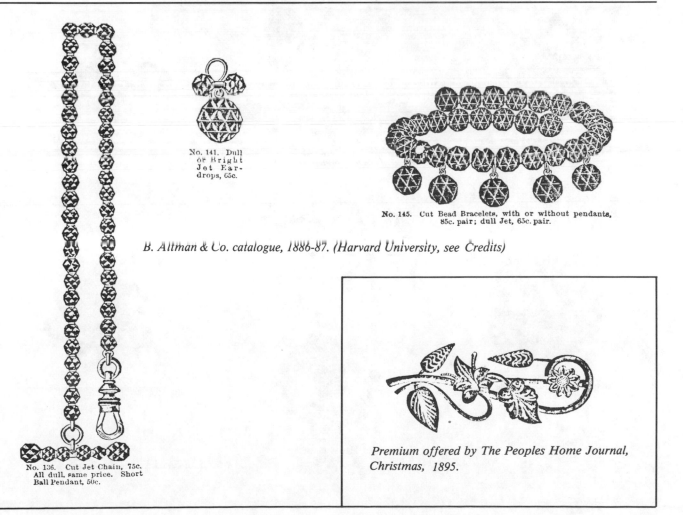

No. 141. Dull or Bright Jet Ear-drops, 65c.

No. 145. Cut Bead Bracelets, with or without pendants, 85c. pair; dull Jet, 65c. pair.

B. Altman & Co. catalogue, 1886-87. (Harvard University, see Credits)

No. 136. Cut Jet Chain, 75c. All dull, same price. Short Ball Pendant, 50c.

Premium offered by The Peoples Home Journal, Christmas, 1895.

BROOCHES, LACE PINS, STICK PINS, AND DROPS.

No. 778.
Matted Finish.
Pearl Settings.
$1 10

No. 779.
Matted Finish.
$0 34

No. 780.
Matted Finish,
Pearl Setting.
$0 67

No. 786.
Matted Finish, Polished Bead Center.
$1 25

No. 904.
$1 00

No. 900.
$0 67

No. 785.
Matted Finish, Pearl Center.
$1 25

No. 787.
Matted Finish, Polished Bead Center.
$1 25

No. 788.
Matted Finish.
$0 75

No. 794.
Matted Finish, Pearl Setting.
$1 30

No. 795.
Matted Finish.
$3 00

No. 792.
Matted Finish, Polished Ball Center.
$1 25

Marshall Field & Co. catalogue, 1896.

B. ALTMAN & CO.—CATALOGUE

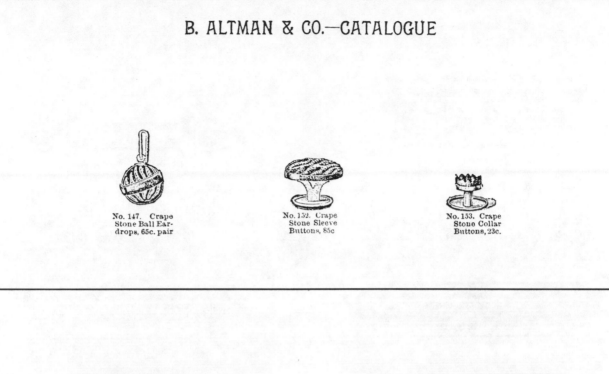

No. 147. Crape
Stone Ball Ear-
drops, 65c. pair

No. 152. Crape
Stone Sleeve
Buttons, 85c

No. 153. Crape
Stone Collar
Buttons, 23c.

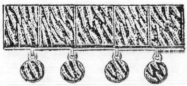

No. 154. Crape Stone Pin, $1.25.

No. 150. Crape Stone Bar Pin, 85c.

No. 142. Crape Stone Ear-
drops, oval or square, 85c.

No. 160. Crape Stone Pin, $1.25.

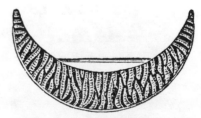

No. 155. Crape Stone Crescent Pin, $1.00.

B. Altman & Co. catalogue, 1886-87.
(Harvard University, see Credits)

B. ALTMAN & CO.—CATALOGUE

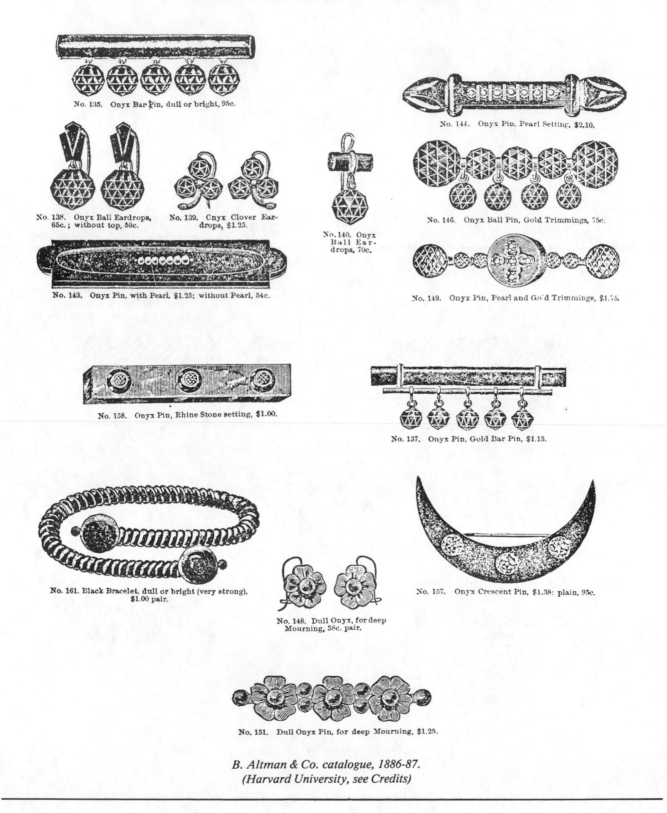

No. 135.   Onyx Bar Pin, dull or bright, 95c.

No. 138.   Onyx Ball Eardrops, 65c.; without top, 50c.

No. 139.   Onyx Clover Eardrops, $1.25.

No. 140.   Onyx Ball Eardrops, 70c.

No. 143.   Onyx Pin, with Pearl, $1.25; without Pearl, 54c.

No. 144.   Onyx Pin, Pearl Setting, $2.10.

No. 146.   Onyx Ball Pin, Gold Trimmings, 75c.

No. 149.   Onyx Pin, Pearl and Go'd Trimmings, $1.75.

No. 158.   Onyx Pin, Rhine Stone setting, $1.00.

No. 137.   Onyx Pin, Gold Bar Pin, $1.15.

No. 161. Black Bracelet, dull or bright (very strong). $1.00 pair.

No. 148.   Dull Onyx, for deep Mourning, 58c. pair.

No. 157.   Onyx Crescent Pin, $1.38; plain, 95c.

No. 151.   Dull Onyx Pin, for deep Mourning, $1.25.

B. Altman & Co. catalogue, 1886-87.
(Harvard University, see Credits)

Onyx brooches, lace pins, stick pins, ear screws and drops, from Marshall Field & Co. catalogues, 1896. (DBI Books, Inc., see Credits)

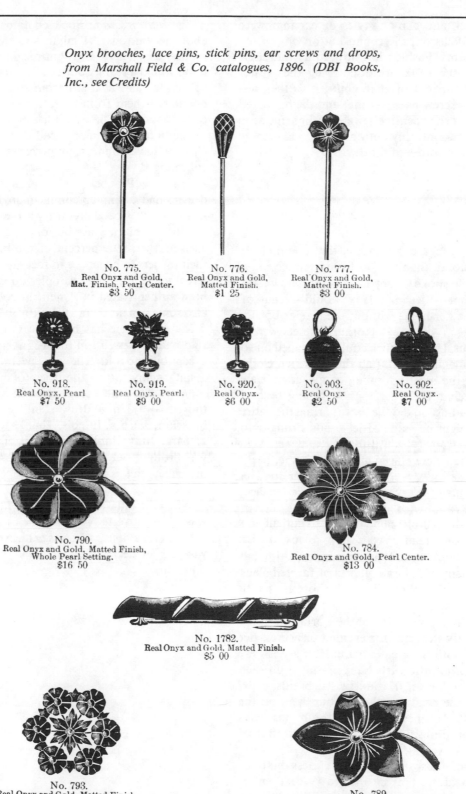

No. 775.
Real Onyx and Gold,
Mat. Finish, Pearl Center.
$3 50

No. 776.
Real Onyx and Gold,
Matted Finish.
$1 25

No. 777.
Real Onyx and Gold,
Matted Finish.
$3 00

No. 918.
Real Onyx, Pearl
$7 50

No. 919.
Real Onyx, Pearl.
$9 00

No. 920.
Real Onyx.
$6 00

No. 903.
Real Onyx
$2 50

No. 902.
Real Onyx.
$7 00

No. 790.
Real Onyx and Gold, Matted Finish,
Whole Pearl Setting.
$16 50

No. 784.
Real Onyx and Gold, Pearl Center.
$13 00

No. 1782.
Real Onyx and Gold, Matted Finish.
$5 00

No. 793.
Real Onyx and Gold, Matted Finish,
Pearl Setting.
$19 00

No 789.
Real Onyx and Gold, Matted Finish.
$11 00

The screw-back and clip-on styles of earrings were worn from the 1920s on, the round button one of the most popular forms. Fashion has now come full circle —the women of the 1970s are discovering the greater comfort pierced earrings offer in contrast to the pressure of the clip or screw-back earring; and the improved safety protects more expensive jewels. Delightful drop earrings, creoles, hoops, tiny button studs and whimsey fashions are now the order of the day.

Hats

"It may be said as regards invention, that one milliner does more in a month than the world of architects in a score of years." So spoke Godey in 1864, and how right he was. No proper Victorian lady would dream of appearing outside her home without the proper bonnet to match her dress. And the Victorian bonnets were a marvel of creation. How so much could be heaped on so little defies the imagination. Of all the Victorian clothing, the hats are the most appealing of all, completely feminine and enchanting. Just as the clothing became laden with jet beading, so did the hats. In time the entire crown of a hat might be made of jet beads strung onto wire, forming a frame; beautiful silks and satins in glowing colors then were placed under the frame, peeking forth in all their glory. Plumes, jetted aigrettes, jet pins and ornaments of every size and shape, jetted lace, jet rain, jet tassels abounded.

At the turn of the century came the hat to end all hats —an enormous one loaded with long black ostrich plumes, jetted aigrettes and jetted coques—with hat pins to match, many with large spheres of faceted black glass. Only Lillian Russel could match those hats with her hourglass figure! The rage for ostrich plumes nearly wiped out the ostrich population of the world.

And when a lady went out for evening pleasures, her hair was dressed with the greatest care. Hair styles were to go from the prim little curls hanging down on each side of the head to bangs, frizzies, twists, braids, coils, piled high upon the head and the low bun worn at the nape of the neck. And nestled among the braids, coils and curls were jet combs, jet star hairpins, butterflies of jet, and jetted lace evening scarves.

The jet mystique also touched black glass buttons, which became fashionable from 1870 to 1910. Then, as now, black glass buttons were advertised as jet. A recently purchased card of black glass buttons was marked "Genuine Jet—Made in Western Germany." Needless to say, an inquiry to the manufacturer brought no response.

The *Button Guide Book* contains this wry comment about jet buttons: "I might add that upon examining thousands of black glass buttons in many places I have never found a real jet button. The real jet buttons in my collection came as a gift from an elderly lady who had purchased them from a craftsman making real jet accessories about 1865 . . . it has been said that 99 percent of the buttons commonly called jet are in reality black glass. I have found that percentage too low for my collecting."

Primrose Peacock, an English author and button dealer, had a similar comment in her book, *Antique Buttons:* "Twice daily I try to explain to would-be vendors of black glass buttons the difference between glass and jet; 99.9 percent of the buttons supposed by their owners to be jet are in fact glass. I have never seen a real jet button, but examples do exist . . . some have been authenticated in American collections. There are also some in a museum at Whitby in Yorkshire."

My experience has been the same in attempting to find true jet jewelry in the Midwest. With one notable exception, no old true jet jewelry has been located despite many, many inquiries to museums across the country. The one exception is the necklace that was tucked away in a drawer in the Aurora Historical Museum, Aurora, Illinois. Thanks to the sharp memory of Mrs. Judy Hankes, assistant curator, the necklace was brought out, inspected and tested. To the best of my belief, this is a true jet necklace dating back to the 1880s.

When the old Tanner House, a landmark in Aurora, was to be converted to the home of the Aurora Historical Society, a house sale was held. Among the items sold was the jet necklace, which was donated back to the museum.

Evening hair dressings from Harper's Bazar, 1894. Bottom right: A jet garniture is used in a coiffure in which the heavily waved hair is drawn back into a small but rather prominent knot composed of puffs and circles. A small cut jet diadem encircles the knot, and two strings of jet cabachons are carried from it across the fluffy front hair.

Jet trimmed hair combs of the 20th Century. Comb on upper right is made of horn and the starburst ornament is on a hinge. Other combs are celluloid.

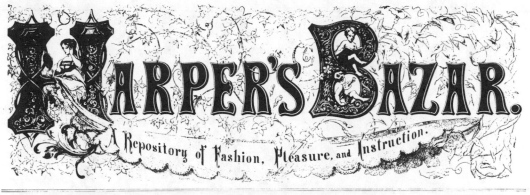

HARPER'S BAZAR.

A Repository of Fashion, Pleasure, and Instruction.

VOL. XIV.—No. 45.
Copyright, 1881, by HARPER & BROTHERS.

NEW YORK, SATURDAY, NOVEMBER 5, 1881.

TEN CENTS A COPY
$4.00 PER YEAR, IN ADVANCE.

*Black straw bonnet with red roses, black plume, black satin
ribbon ties, jet ornament on crown (jet trim on cloak), from
Harper's Bazar, 1881.*

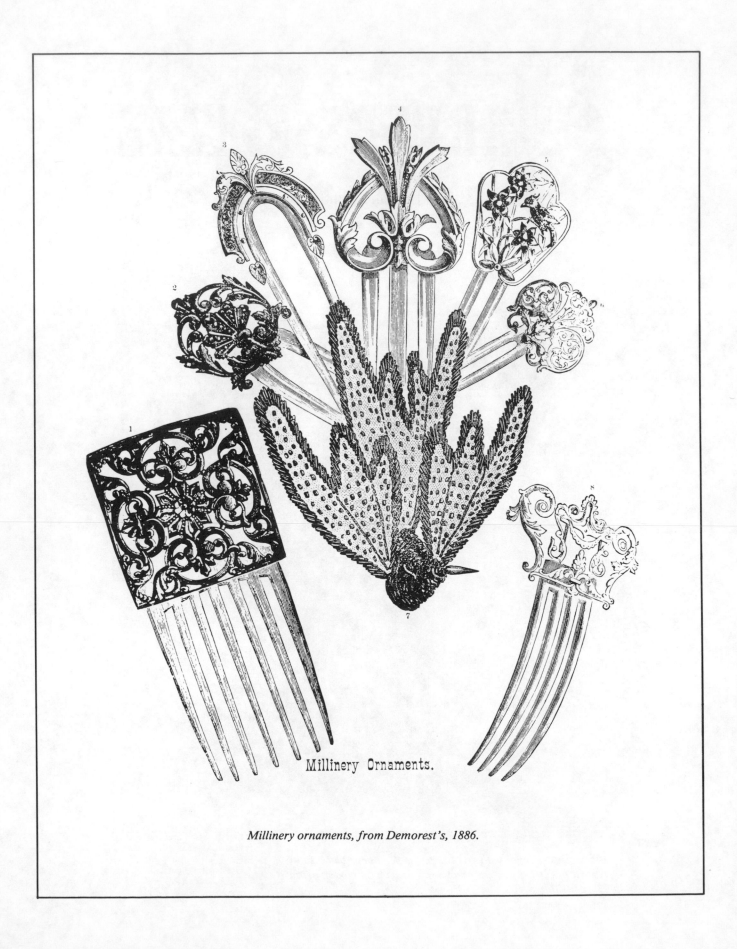

Millinery Ornaments.

Millinery ornaments, from Demorest's, 1886.

Bonnets and parasols, from Harper's Bazar, 1892.

BONNETS AND PARASOLS

Fig. a: jet bonnet.
Fig. b: jet bonnet.
Fig. c: jet bonnet frame.
Fig. d: jet bonnet frame.
Fig. e: hat for girl from 4 to 6 years old.
Fig. f: girl's sailor hat.
Fig. g: breakfast cap.
Fig. h: parasols.

Black silk toque with a coronet of black jet set above brim and a single yellow rose, from The Delineator, 1891.

Rear view of bonnet with jet edging at back and edge of front rim, from Peterson's, 1887.

Black velvet toque with jetted lace and chrysanthemums and yellow satin ribbons (left); puckered dark red velvet toque, with jet coronet and jet stars on each side of center knot (right); from Peterson's, 1890.

Wire-mounted brooch, c. 1900s (top); heavy wire hair barrette, c. 1890s (center); wire-mounted tiara, c. 1890s, with small rings at each end for fastening of elastic.

Jet hat ornaments, c. 1890s.

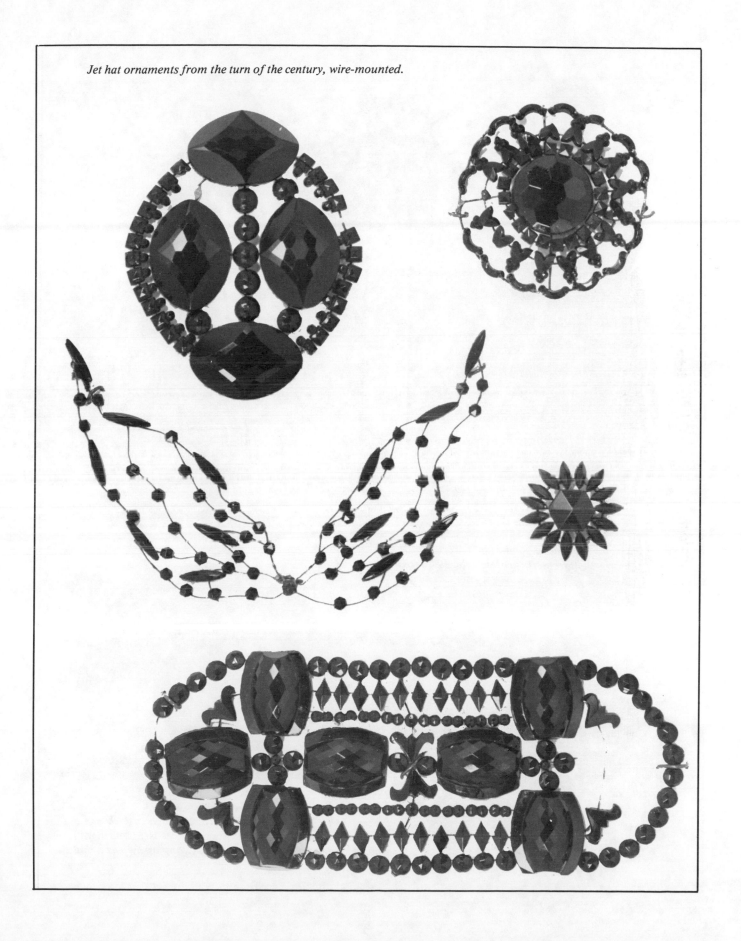

Jet hat ornaments from the turn of the century, wire-mounted.

*Hair pins: jet beaded bonnet pin, c. 1880s (left);
jet hair ornament (center); Art Deco pin, 1930s (right).*

*Passementerie hat ornaments, c. 1880s. Each brooch has a
perforated metal back to which each facet is fastened with
wire. All have simple "C" clasps. The long arrow has a dull
finish.*

Jet trimmed hat pins, c. 1890s.

Jetted hat aigrettes, c. 1890s.

Buttons

True jet adapted itself beautifully to large chunky shapes. While some buttons undoubtedly were made, along with carved medallions and lockets, the quantity probably was small. Particularly after the changeover to Spanish jet at Whitby, the number of jet buttons made must have been reduced considerably. Further, true jet would have been impractical for buttons in light of the much harder wear they receive. Those few made may have been produced as a special gift out of scraps too small to be used for the larger pieces of jewelry.

Although some glass buttons were made in France and Germany (and today many fine black glass buttons come from Germany) most of the black glass buttons of the Victorian era probably were products of Bohemia. Nowhere in the whole field of black glass is the artistry of the glassmaker more apparent than in the buttons. Finishes ranged from mirror-like to completely dull. Copper, gold and silver lusters were used as a complete wash over the face, or as trim. The silver luster buttons are sometimes thought to be of steel, which they were made to imitate; their brilliance was caused by the use of platinum. Designs were etched or molded into the face, gold and/or silver placed into the etched lines, and the entire button again fired for permanence. Some black glass buttons were painted so delicately that they looked more like fabric than glass.

Victorian ladies were quite serious about their buttons, regarding them as important as their jewelry. After Queen Victoria chose them for personal wear, black glass buttons were a sign of good taste, correct for all time. In keeping with the traditions of the time, buttons were made expressly for mourning clothes; for the first mourning the finish was dull; after the proper interval of time had passed, half mourning buttons were appropriate for use, and generally were a combination of a dull and bright finish. As the craze for jet beadwork mounted, so did the use of the black glass button to compliment it.

The classical Greek gods and goddesses seen on brooches also were favorite subjects of the button makers. Again, Athena stole the show.

The black glass button most familiar to American women today is the faceted black button, ranging in size from very small to the size of a half dollar, and varying in shape from round to square, diamond, oval, crescent and oblong. In 1879, Worth used buttons of smooth polished jet the size of a silver dollar, sewn through two gold-rimmed eyes that ornamented the center. He also covered molds with fabric, mounted the mold to metal and set it all into a rim of jet. Button collectors refer to this type, with the metal rim, as a Victorian jewel. These

were the largest and fanciest of all, used on opera cloaks and fur wraps. The jewel usually was a three-part button—the metal back and the shank, the glass center, and the rim holding the entire button together. With their fancy rims and sparkling glass centers, the large jewels must have been spectacular on the outer wraps.

The fashion columns of the old periodicals were marvels in their minute and detailed descriptions of the latest styles, fabrics and millinery—the fashion plates were pure delights. Unfortunately, jewelry illustrations are not easily found. Those that have been unearthed are treated as pure treasure, for they help to understand more thoroughly the written description, and form the basis of a time sequence.

The fashion columns were equally generous in their mention of the House of Worth, local dressmaking establishments, fabric houses and department stores. But jewelry sources or designer names were conspicuously absent.

The 19th Century produced many fine jewelry designer/craftsmen—Italy's Castellani and Giulliano; England's Ashbee, Gilbert, Eastlake; France's Lalique, Mucha, Boucheron; America's Tiffany. One of the few designer references found was an illustration from the 1872 *Art Journal* entitled "Black Glass Jewelry by William Whitely." These were exquisitely designed brooches and pendants, in the Grand Style, of Gothic influence. The truth probably is that the leading designers were much too busy producing the expensive jewels for the wealthy; further, these designers would not have wanted their names connected with the common black glass jewelry since it might have been considered harmful to their prestige. Their influence, however, would have filtered down, just as the House of Worth placed its stamp upon the fashions of the time.

Although the black glass was a cheaper, mass-produced item, it actually was quite attractive. The old black glass—though much of it is now chipped or broken with settings bent and rusted—has a certain charm. Perhaps the time has come to honor black glass in its own right, to lift it from the shadow of the jet mystique and give it an honorable place of its own.

(See Appendix II for information on testing Victorian jewelry.)

BUTTON GAUGE.

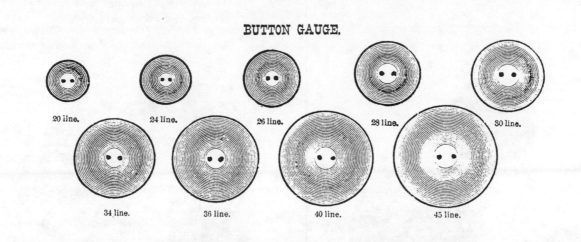

20 line.   24 line.   26 line.   28 line.   30 line.

34 line.   36 line.   40 line.   45 line.

Button gauge, from B. Altman & Co. catalogue, 1879-80.

Dress and Cloak Buttons.

No. 1.   No. 2.   No. 3.   No. 4.   No. 5.   No. 6.   No. 7.   No. 8.   No. 9.

No. 10.   No. 11.   No. 12.   No. 13.   No. 12.   No. 13.   No. 14.   No. 15.   No. 16.

No.	DRESS AND CLOAK BUTTONS.	Line.	4½	5	5½	6	6½	7	7½	12	14	15	16
1	Fine Black Silk, Fancy Crochet Ball Button.......... per dozen.		18	22	..	..	..	..	..	..	..	..	..
2	Fine Black Silk, Fancy Crochet Button, Watch Shape........ "		..	..	28	32	..	..	..	..	..	..	..
3	Fine Black Silk Crochet Button, with Cut Jet Bead Centre, Watch Shape.......... "		..	..	..	22	25	..	..	..	..	..	..
4	Fine Black Silk Crochet Ball Button, with Cut Jet Bead Centre .... "		28	30	..	..	..	..	..	..	..	..	..
5	Fine Black Cut Jet Ball Button.................... "		22	..	..	..	..	..	..	..	..	..	..
6	Fine Black Flat Cut Jet Button.................... "		..	..	..	..	30	..	..	..	..	..	..
7	Fine Fancy Black Flat Jet Button.................... "		..	..	..	..	15	..	..	..	..	..	..
8	Fine Black Fancy Dull Jet Button.................... "		..	..	..	..	..	20	..	..	..	..	..
9	Steel Button, with Cut Steel Point Centre, Bronze, Garnet, Steel, Blue........... "		..	..	..	..	28	..	..	..	..	•	..
10	Steel Button, with Fancy Metal Centre, Green, Black, Blue, Garnet, Brown, Oxidized, Light Bronze, Medium Bronze......... "		..	•.	..	..	25	..	..	45	..	..	..
11	Fancy Metal Button with Cut Steel Point, Bronze, Brown, Garnet, Blue, Oxidized.......... "		..	..	..	..	..	..	30	..	..	..	90
12	Fancy Metal Button, Bronze, Brown, Garnet, Blue, Green, Olive........ "		..	..	..	..	..	..	20	..	..	..	..
13	Fancy Steel Button with Cut Steel Point Centre, Bronze, Oxidized, Brown, Garnet, Blue, Green "		..	..	..	..	35	..	..	..	..	..	..
14	Fancy Metal Button with Cut Steel Points, Oxidized, Steel, Bronze, Brown, Garnet, Blue, Green "		..	..	..	..	..	45	..	85	..	..	..
15	Fancy Metal Button with Cut Steel Points, Oxidized, Bronze, Brown, Old Silver, Black and Steel................. "		..	..	..	..	..	58	..	1.00	..	..	..
16	Fancy Metal Button with Cut Steel Points, Oxidized, Bronze, Brown, Black............... "		..	..	..	..	..	68	..	..	..	..	..
17	Fancy Metal Button with Cut Steel Points, Bronze, Steel and Oxidized .... "		..	..	..	..	..	65	..	1.55	..	..	..
18	Fancy Metal Button with Steel Points, Oxidized, Bronze, Brown, Oxidized Silver........... "		..	..	..	..	..	42	..	..	85	..	..

Dress and cloak buttons, from
B. Altman & Co. catalogue, 1886-87.

Victorian jewel buttons with brass settings and black glass centers.

Molded black glass buttons with the fabric look.

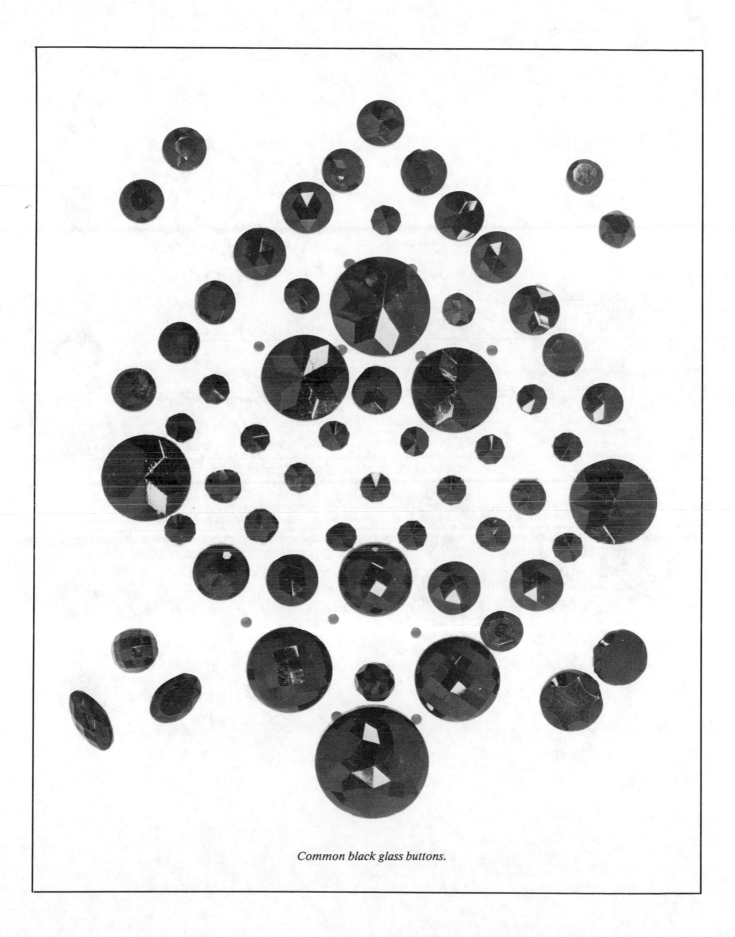

Common black glass buttons.

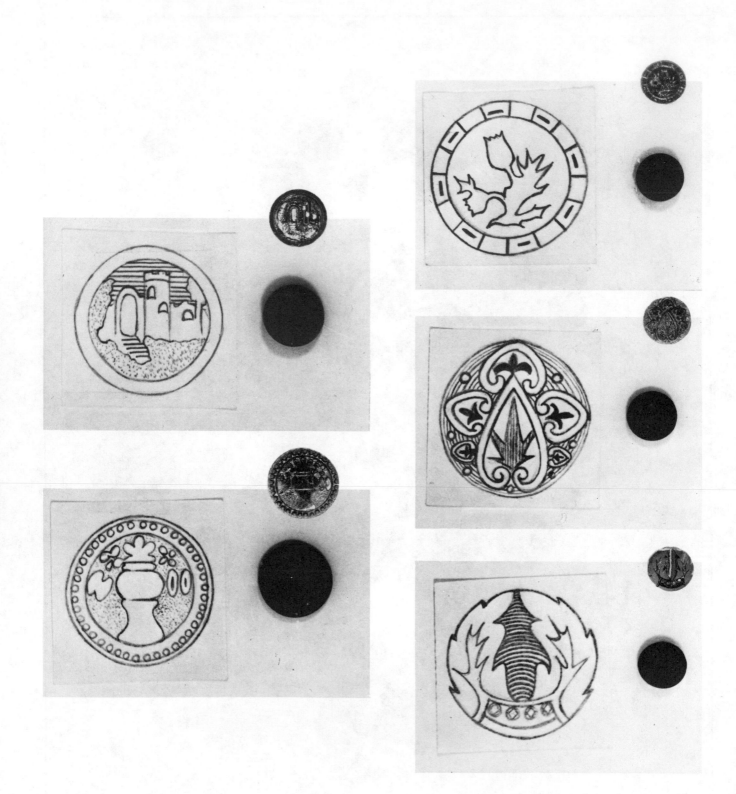

Black glass buttons, c. 1880-1900.

Black glass of the Art Deco period, 1930s.

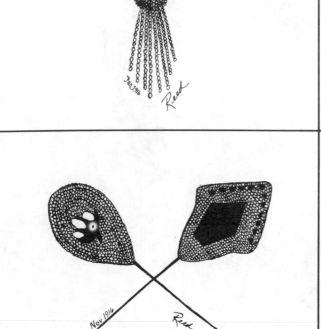

Sketches from the pages of the Ladies' Home Journal. Top left: jet beaded hat ornament. Top right: jet beaded butterfly hat ornament. Center left: jet beaded hat pins. Center right: crystal and jet hat pins. Bottom left: jet tassel. (Downe Publishing Co., see Credits.)

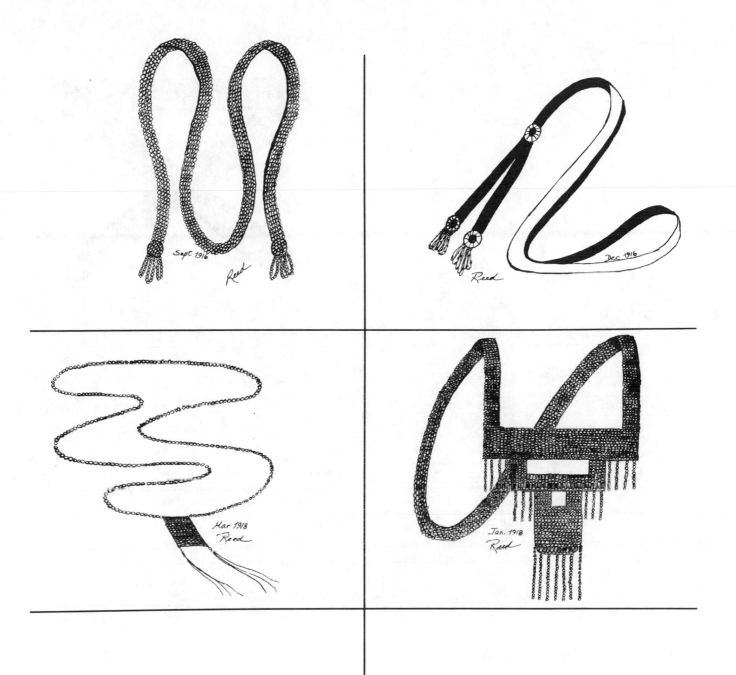

Jet necklaces.

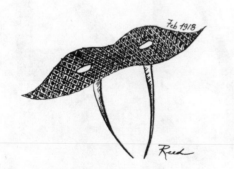

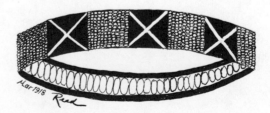

Sketches from the pages of the Ladies' Home Journal. Top right: jet beaded head band. Center left: jet hair comb. Bottom left: jet bead chain. Bottom right: jet bracelet. (Downe Publishing Co., see Credits)

Onyx

The use of onyx during Victorian times could have stemmed from the religious significance that onyx held. Mentioned in Genesis, Exodus and Job, onyx was among the 12 precious stones set on the breastplate of the high priest, each one engraved with the name of one of the sons of Jacob. Being the eleventh stone, the onyx bore the name of Joseph. Also in onyx were two stones, set in couches of gold and placed on the shoulders of the ephod (short sleeveless cloak of the high priest), with the names of the children of Israel engraved upon them—six names on one stone, six on the other.

In its natural state, onyx has parallel layers of different colors; it was used in carved cameos. Pliny asserted the word "onyx" derived from "a nail": "because it hath a white in it resembling that in the nail of a man's finger."

A special line of mourning jewelry was created and patented by the Fowler Brothers of Providence, Rhode Island, about 1874. Fowler's English Crape Stone jewelry was marketed in the United States, England, France, Belgium and Austria-Hungary. The onyx was cut to shape with tools and abraded with acids to produce a line effect, then colored to produce a dull black finish. Some of the onyx was purchased from the western territories of the United States, then sent to Germany where it was cut into the desired shapes. Other onyx came from Idar, Oldenburg—the "craping" treatment completed in the Providence shop.

Secondary crape stone was made of black glass, molded to the desired shapes; it was covered with a film of wax at certain points, then placed into a bath of corrosive acid which produced the crape or line effect. The onyx jewelry shown from the Altman & Company catalogue could very easily be a combination of onyx and black glass, the beads used as drops made of black glass.

The use of jet in ornaments was not confined to the continent of Europe or England. On the continent of America, jet has been used by the Southwestern Indians in ages past, and is still in use today.

The National Geographic Society began extensive exploration of Pueblo Bonito in 1921. Located in the Chaco Canyon National Monument in the northwestern corner of New Mexico, Pueblo Bonito was a large village that once sheltered more than 1,200 people. Dating of this village is set at 500 years before Columbus sailed to find a new world. Among the many finds was a small frog carved of jet, with a turquoise collar and turquoise eyes.

The Zuni call jet "black turquoise," and use it along with coral, shell and turquoise in their jewelry making. Some of the best jet of the Southwest comes from the Acoma (from Akome "People of the White Rock") reservation. The Acoma Pueblo is located on a mesa 357 feet high about 60 miles west of the Rio Grande. It was first mentioned as "Acus" by Marcos de Niza in 1539 and visited by Coronado in 1540. In prehistoric times, the Acomas lived on the summit of an even higher mesa, known as Katzima, or the "Enchanted Mesa" three miles northeastward.

JEWELRY AND TRIMMINGS

15

The Horns of Plenty

The horns of animals on the hoof may not seem overly appealing; in the hands of a craftsman, however, animal horn assumes another dimension. As with so many of our antiquities, the origins are lost—we can only speculate as to when early man decided the animal horn would make a fine drinking cup. When the art of carving came into being, the horn was ornately decorated; in time it was trimmed with brass and silver. The horn cup was valued highly since the ancients believed it had the power to reveal poison. Homer described the bow of Pandarus as two horns of a wild goat fastened together at the base and tipped with gold. Early Chinese bows were made partly of wood and partly of buffalo horn; West Indian bows were made of horn and wood strapped together with a tendon. Horn was used as barter, and Marco Polo brought Kubla Kahn rhinoceros horn as a gesture of tribute. The Vikings covered the stocks of their broadswords with wood or horn. The horns that called villagers together usually were ordinary cow horns, similar to the ancient Shofar or booming ram's horn. Complete suits of scale armor were made of horn and worn by the Arabians for protection in battle. Old lanterns were called lanthorns because the sides were set with horn panes, although there is some question as to how functional such panes could have been.

Long ago, horn was used as a protective covering for manuscript labels. The title was written on parchment or vellum, then covered with a thin plate of horn. The next step was to fasten these to the cover of the manuscript with brass tacks. Wood, covered with leather, often formed the outer binding of the manuscripts, with leather or thin brass strips laid at the edges of the horn sheet to give extra protection. This may have inspired the development of the horn book for children, which generally was used only in England and America.

The book actually was a small, square-shaped wooden paddle, with the ABC's written on parchment or vellum fastened to one side of the paddle. To protect the parchment from grubby little fingers, a covering of translucent horn was placed over the parchment. The edges were bound with thin strips of brass, or latten, held in place with rose head nails. A small hole was drilled in the handle of the paddle, strung with a leather thong, which could be tied around the child's waist—no excuse to forget the book this way. In the early days of the colonies, the horn books were imported from England, and there is evidence the Pilgrim children not only learned their ABC's from them, but the Lord's Prayer as well.

Combs

The early colonies had hornsmiths among their craftsmen, who, in reality, were comb makers. To obtain his supply of horn, the hornsmith simply saddled his horse and made the rounds of the farms in the area. Farmers saved the horns for just such an opportunity; the hornsmith picked those most suitable for use, loaded up the saddle bags and went on his way. The earliest combs in this country were cut from what was known as raw horn —horn flattened out with its original color untouched. Since most of the hornsmiths usually were farmers, too, an ordinary farm saw was used to cut the teeth into the comb, which resulted in some rather crude combs, irregular in shape.

Crude or not, combs were very valuable—particularly those made of tortoise shell. Horn became a substitute for the expensive shell—the poor man's shell. When a comb was damaged it was taken to a comb shop where, for six cents, it was repaired, polished and guaranteed for strength.

In preparing horn for use, the hornsmith cut off the solid tips; the balance of the horn was hollow with a bony inner core (pith). This was soaked in cold water for several weeks to separate the pith from the pure horn. After this, the horn itself was split lengthways, and pressed cold between iron plates to form flat sheets. In the early days of comb making it was customary to cut up the horn, press it, make the combs and wrap them, all in one day. For a while, horn was softened in whale oil, until that became too expensive. Hot water was then substituted in the softening process.

In these early days "trampin jours" or journey men often were part-time comb makers. The "jours" walked through the country with their kits of tools slung over their shoulders, looking for work. Stopping at various comb shops along the way, they worked for a week or so until there was no work, or simply would pick up and leave when their feet began to itch.

Buttons

The first American buttonmaker known to have used horn is Enoch Noyes, who practiced his craft in 1759 at West Newbury, Massachusetts. Working in a little shop in his home, he concentrated mainly on comb making: the buttons probably were just a sideline—no doubt to use up the solid tips of the horns.

Among the early written records of horn buttons on the frontier is that of John Askin, a Scotch-Irish trader who had settled in Fort Michilimackinac in 1764. A very thorough businessman, John took a meticulous inventory of his stock on December 31, 1778. Included in the listing were six and a half dozen horn buttons and 14 corn combs—both probably destined as gifts to the Indians.

All of the trade goods for the fort came by boat from Montreal and Quebec, which in turn obtained their trade goods from England. The first record of any patent issued in connection with combs is that of Isaac Tryon of Connecticut, a soldier of the revolution, who made combs on a machine of his own invention, patented in 1798.

Enoch Noyes' establishment in West Newbury made the small farm community the first comb making center in the New World. As the demand for combs grew, the farmers began to farm less and devote more time to the making of combs, either in their homes or in small shops. Hornsmithing was slow hard work, with small profits and low wages. A fortunate journeyman could earn a dollar a day, but at times, this was more than farming paid. As with so many of the trade guilds, the only way to enter the hornsmithing craft was through an apprenticeship. The apprentices were expected to work every day—holidays were the only exception—from the middle of September to the middle of March. Two terms of schooling, each three months long, were allowed. The apprentice could not be out after nine o'clock in the evening, was expected to attend church twice on Sunday and to spend Saturday evening preparing for Sunday school. If the apprentice were really lucky, he might find an employer who would give extra money for clothing purchases. Other than that, he worked as required, received his hornsmith training and room and board, which usually promised the plainest of food.

The cottage-industry concept was applied to the final touches on the combs. The completed combs were distributed among the women of the village for bending and polishing. The horn combs were polished by rubbing with common charcoal ashes moistened with water. To bend them, the combs were slightly warmed, then tied over a long, rounded arm of wood. After one side of the arm was filled, the arm was turned so the worker could fill the other side. By this time, the first batch was ready to be removed. Later, the bending process was improved with sets of blocks, properly curved. The warm comb was placed between the blocks, which were then locked together.

Since the tortoise shell comb was so highly prized, its imitation—made of horn—was not long in arriving. A man and wife in West Newbury specialized in coloring the horn; a paste was made of lime, saleratus and litharge, mixed according to judgment and allowed to stand for 24 hours. The combs were placed on a board and spattered with a feather dipped into the mixture. After the coloring had dried, the combs were washed. The

Natural and dyed horn buttons.

Mourning pins of dyed animal horn, c. 1870-1890. All have simple "C" clasps, with black glass beads used either as holding pins or trim.

result was a tortoise shell effect, the success of the imitation depending upon the skill of the spatterer. Amber effects were obtained by dipping the combs in aqua fortis; black was obtained by using sugar of lead.

As comb making in Massachusetts became an important skill, in 1774 the Provincial Congress of Massachusetts recommended that its people encourage hornsmiths. The Revolutionary War gave impetus to the movement since comb imports from the Old World virtually ceased. Whether the fortunes of war or itchy feet were the cause, some of the West Newbury residents decided to move to Leominster, Massachusetts, to open comb making shops in that city. In time, Leominster became *the* comb making center of the United States.

The processing of horn remained basically the same until about 1805, when a clarifying process was discovered. In this process, the horn was covered with pieces of tallow, then pressed between hot irons, which gave a clearer or more transparent quality to the horn. A descendant of Enoch Noyes, David Noyes, invented a clarifying press in 1824 that shortened production time and produced an even clearer horn. The demand for fancy hair combs was increasing and the clearer horn adapted itself to the latest style beautifully.

By the 1840s steam began to replace the old sweep horsepower, and fashion demands were forcing manufacturers to keep alert and develop new ideas. By 1850, Leominster was leading in the comb industry; one newspaper stated that two-thirds of the combs manufactured in the United States were made in Leominster. At this time, the average comb maker received one dollar for a 10-hour day, but the most expert, by spending from 12 to 15 hours on piecework often doubled that sum. Women were allowed three dollars a week. Both men and women paid board out of their wages; the men $2.25 weekly, the women $1.50 weekly.

Soon, bonnet pins were added to the production line; the wee little hats that perched on top the head, tied with bonnet strings under the chin, were very easily blown away. Horn pins, four or five inches in length were developed; the ends were sharpened and the center was twisted like the threads of a screw. The sharp points made it easy to push the pin through the coils of hair and into the bonnet, while the twisted center prevented the pin from slipping out of the hair.

During the Civil War years, and the years immediately following, the whole world seemed to want horn jewelry and novelties. In those days, the horn watch chain was particularly popular, the favorite length being about 54 inches. All the comb shops in Leominster worked to capacity trying to meet the demand. It was not unusual for jewelry agents from all over the country to haunt the shops day and night, often snatching uncompleted chains from the racks. Button making's secondary status was emphasized by the fact that a man named James Grove of England supplied horn buttons for both the federal and confederate armies during the Civil War.

While the American hornsmiths were busy developing their comb industry, in France Emile Bassot was bringing horn button making to a high degree of perfection. He is credited with the invention of the molded horn process, which he also introduced in England. Utilizing the hooves of cattle, the processed, liquefied horn was poured into molds. For buttons, the wire shanks were inserted into the molds. Until the time of his death in 1864, Bassot was considered the greatest authority on horn button making in France. English button makers, visiting the Paris Exhibition in 1867, had to swallow their pride and admit the superiority of the French mold makers: "The very fine classical heads upon some of the buttons in alto relievo show a great amount of skill in the execution of the dies," and "they are masterpieces in the art of die sinking. The heads which are very deep, have the appearance of being undercut, although this is not so."

In preparation for the molds, the hooves were boiled until soft and cut into halves, from which blanks were cut. The blanks were then placed into vats containing strong dye—red, green or black. From the vat the blanks moved to the mold table, where the lower halves of a dozen molds were set into an iron box. The hoof blanks were placed into the molds and the entire box slid into an oven, where the hooves were heated to the softness of wax. At this point the top half of the mold was set, which usually contained the pattern for the ornament. The molds then were placed into a press that completed forming the ornament. After removal from the mold, the ornaments were cleaned and polished—ready for sale. Whether the ornament was made of horn or hoof, it usually was billed as a horn product.

With the cessation of the Civil War in America, the horn button trade in England declined and James Grove found himself in financial trouble. Being a very determined man, he decided to go into the production of dyed horn ornaments and brooches, which sold on the market as imitation jet. The jet mystique emerged again.

But two developments were looming on the horizon that eventually would change the horn industry dramatically. The first was the increasing rarity of natural horn—the second was one man's fondness for the game of billiards. On learning that the ivory billiard ball was scarce and very costly, John Hyatt began the search for a substitute. Possessing a general knowledge of chemistry, an affinity for mechanics and an inventive streak, Hyatt began to experiment, eventually producing the

This dyed horn locket (c. 1870s) is an exquisitely detailed sample of the art of fine die sinking. The locket opens on the right. In the bottom half, an oval brass-rim frame for a photograph is recessed into the body, surrounded by a garland of flowers slightly raised on the surface of the horn. The head is affixed to the face of the locket.

product called *Celluloid*, which he patented in 1873.

While Hyatt experimented with his ivory substitute, cattle were being dehorned at an alarming rate. By the 1890s the situation became critical, and American hornsmiths began searching the world over to find additional supplies of horn. European horn, with the exception of small quantities of English and Australian stock, proved unsuitable. South America was investigated and a good supply of horn was found there; agencies to procure it were established in Argentina and Uruguay—but even this was not enough to supply the horn needed to keep up with a flourishing industry. Finally, experiments

were started with celluloid, and the transition from horn to the new material took place between 1895 and 1900. The need for a horn substitute was the springboard for the plastics industry that is so much a part of modern life.

René Lalique of France gave horn its final salute. Active in the Art Nouveau movement that began in Paris in the mid-1890s, Lalique shaped horn combs in a dramatic and flowing pattern. The upper sections of the combs frequently were set with semi-precious stones and obsidian, a far cry from the ornately carved high Spanish-style combs so greatly used during the Victorian era. In later years, Lalique turned from jewelry designing to glassmaking, producing strikingly beautiful perfume bottles for Coty.

While the firm started by James Grove in England still produces horn buttons, horn jewelry and combs have joined the ranks of the antiquities, along with true jet. Today, natural horn buttons are made by home craftsmen, along with some sculpture using the natural line of the horn as a medium of expression.

The jet mystique has come full circle; Whitby jet was nosed out by Spanish jet, and black glass imitated both of them. Black garnets, obsidian and onyx were liberally sprinkled in between. Horn was made to imitate jet, and then replaced by celluloid. Truth in advertising was an unknown commodity during Victorian times, and the ladies of that time must indeed have had some difficulties in knowing exactly what they were buying. The surviving trinkets and treasures remind us gently of a very special era of America that will never pass this way again.

A variety of quartz has been named hornstone, dubbed so by the miners, because of its tenacity which resembled that of a horn or horse's hoof. This stone generally was gray and tinged blue, green, brown or yellow. Some of it had the quality of being translucent, other opaque. It sometimes was found embedded in limestone, as in the Tyrol; in viens in Hungary and Sweden, and in pseudomorphs in Saxony and Bohemia. The material was used for snuff boxes, seals and mortars, but chiefly for the handles of knives and forks. It was exported from Germany in large quantities for mounting butter and dessert knives.

(From Bristow's Glossary of Minerology—1861.)

APPENDIX I:

AMERICAN PUBLISHERS OF FASHION PLATES

	Start of Publication	Ceased Publication
The Casket	1826	1840*
Ladies Magazine (Sarah Hale)	1828	1837**
– Ladies Magazine (Godey)	1830	1898
Snowden's Ladies Companion	1834	1844**
– Graham's	1840	1858
Miss Leslie's Magazine	1843	1846**
– Columbian Magazine	1844	1849
– Peterson's	1842	1898
Arthur's	1850	1898
– Harper's Monthly Magazine	1850	1864
– Leslie Publications	1857	1882
– Demorest Publications	1860	1899
Ladies Quarterly Report/Metropolitan (Butterick)	1864	1872
– Harper's Bazar	1867	
– Ladies Own Magazine	1869	1874
– Delineator	1872	1937
Queen/McCall's Magazine	1872	
Woman's Home Companion	1873	
Ladies Home Journal	1883	
Good Housekeeping	1885	

  * Name changed to Graham's

** Merged with Godey's

 – Examples contained in the illustrations

APPENDIX II:

COMPARATIVE RANKS ON MOH'S SCALE OF HARDNESS

	Hardness	Density	Refractive Index
Garnet family:			
Almandine Garnets	7.50	3.95	
Andradite or black melanite garnets	7.25	3.90	1:89
Pyrope—red	7.25	3.65	1:73
Glass	6	4.20-2.	1:70-1:44
Obsidian	5	2.33-2.42	1:50
Jet	4.0-2.5	1:33	1:66
Horn	2.5	1:70-1.85	1:56
Amber	2.0		1:54
Celluloid	2.0	1.35	1:495-1:520

Black garnets—a variety of iron lime garnet, of a velvet black color. Located in Norway, the Pyrenees, the older lavas of Vesuvius and the papal states of St. Albano and Frascat, near Rome, the latter locally called Black Garnets of Frascati.

Obsidian—A volcanic glass, produced by fusion of felspathic rocks or those containing or composed of alkaline silicates; hence the composition is very variable. Generally black and opaque mass; in the 1860s it was converted into snuff boxes, knife handles and into various articles of mourning jewelry. Found in Victorian era in Iceland, Siberia, Hungary, Mexico, Peru, islands of the Greek Archipelago.

Black Amber—was the name given by the Prussian amber diggers to jet, because it was found accompanying amber. Amber was found along Baltic coast, Sicilian coast, in clay near Paris, and occasionally on the sea coasts of Norfolk, Essex, Sussex and Kent.

Jet [ture]—A variety of lignite. Color velvet black or brownish black when passing into bituminous wood. Brilliant luster and resinous. Sectile and brittle. Feels remarkably smooth; does not stain the fingers; slightly heavier than water

Volatile matter ....37.90 percent

Ash ....1.70 percent

Carbon ....61.40 percent

Testing Methods

The high density reading of black melanite garnets and the negative reading shown when the stones are tested on a standard refractometer will distinguish the black garnets from black tourmaline, black-stained chalcedony (onxy stained black) or black glass.

The "burn" test used to determine the nature of a material. Glass, obsidian and garnets would not, of course, burn. Jet burns with a greenish flame and emits a sweetish bituminous smell, leaving a light yellowish-colored ash. Amber burns with a yellow flame, emits an agreeable odor and leaves a black, shining, light carbonaceous residue. Horn will burn with a most disagreeable odor—that of burning feathers or hair. Celluloid emits an acid odor; one button put to the test burned to a crisp ash in less than one minute.

The simplest method is to use a long, strong pin, heated to red hot on the tip. Insert it into the back of the ornament. The smell that emanates from horn and celluloid is unmistakable, and the hot pin enters the material most easily. Jet, a much harder substance, will not accept the hot pin easily, and will emit very little odor. Jet is altered wood, and the veins of jet frequently resemble the shape of tree branches.

Bibliography

Agricola, Georgius, *De Re Metallica*, translated from the first Latin edition of 1556 by Herbert G. Hoover and Lou B. Hoover in 1912, published by Dover Publications, 1950.

Albert, Kent, *Complete Button Book*, published 1949, reprint 1971, John Edwards, Publisher, Appledore, Stratford, Conn.

American Life Foundation, *Button Guide*, Books 1 and 2, published 1972, American Life Foundation, Watkins Glen, N.Y. Distributed by Century House, Watkins Glen, N.Y.

Bordeux, Jeanne, *Eleanora Duse: The Story of Her Life*, 5th Edition, George H. Doran Co.

Bristow, Henry, *A Glossary of Minerology*, Longman, Green, Longman and Roberts, published in London, 1861.

Burke, John, *Duet In Diamonds*, published 1972, 2nd Edition, G.P. Putnam's Sons, New York.

Coarelli, Filippo, *Greek and Roman Jewelry*, translated by Dr. D. Strong, Hamlyn Publishing Group Limited, Hamlyn House, Feltham, Middlesex, England, 1970.

Cooper & Batterskill, *Victorian Sentimental Jewelry*, A.S. Barnes & Co., New Jersey, 1972.

Curran, Mona, *Collecting Antique Jewelry*, 2nd Edition, 1970, Emerson Books, Buchanam, N.Y.

Doyle, Bernard W., *Comb Making in America—An Account of the Origin and Development of the Industry for which Leominster has Become Famous*, privately printed in commemoration of the 150th anniversary of the founding of the comb industry in Leominster, Mass., 1925.

Earle, Alice Morse, *Two Centuries of Costume in America 1620-1820*, originally published by the Macmillan Co., New York, 1902; published with minor corrections in 1970, Dover Publications, New York.

Evans, Mary, A.M., *Costume Throughout The Ages*, J.B. Lippincott Co., 1920.

Finley, Ruth E., *The Lady of Godey's: Sarah Josepha Hale*, 3rd Edition, 1931, J.B. Lippincott Co., Philadelphia.

Ford, Grace Horney, *The Button Collector's History*, 1943, Pond Ekberg Co., Springfield, Mass., to be republished 1976 by The New England Publishing Co., Stratford, Conn.

Fregnac, Claude, *Jewelry*, Octopus Books Ltd., 1st Edition, 1973, London.

Gerson, Noel, *Because I Loved Him*, William Morrow & Co., 1971, Reader's Digest Condensed Version.

Giles, Dorothy, *Road Thru Czechoslovakia*, 1930, Penn Publishing Co., Philadelphia.

Harrigton, J.C., *Glassmaking at Jamestown*, Dietz Press, 1952, Richmond, Va.

Holbrook, Stewart H., *The Age of the Moguls*, 1953, Country Life Press.

Hugo, Victor, *Les Miserables*, translated by Lascelles Wraxall, 1938, Heritage Press.

Jones, Mary Harris, *The Autobiography of Mother Jones*, edited by Mary Field Parton, 1972, Charles H. Kerr Publishing Company for the Illinois Labor History Society, Chicago, Ill.

Jones, W. Unite, *The Button Industry*, 1924, Sir Isaac Pitman & Sons, London.

Knittle, Rhea Mansfield, *Early American Glass*, 1927, The Century Co., New York.

La Gallienne, Eva, *The Mystic in the Theatre*, 1973, Southern Illinois University Press.

Lester, Katherine Morris, *Historic Costumes*, 1933, The Manual Arts Press, Peoria, Ill.

McClellan, Elizabeth, *History of American Costume*, (3rd Edition), 1937, Tudor Publishing Co.; first edition, 1902, George W. Jacobs & Co.

Macquitty, William, *Tutankhamun, The Last Journey*, 1972, Sphere Books Ltd., Great Britain.

Moore, Doris Langley, *Fashions Thru Fashion Plates*, First American Edition, 1971, Clarkson N. Potter, Inc., New York.

Moore, Elwood S., *Coal*, 1922, John Wiley and Sons.

Moore, N.H., *Old Glass*, 1924, Frederick A. Stokes Co.

Mott, Luther, *A History of American Magazines*, Vol. I-IV, 1957, Harvard University Press.

Peacock, Primrose, *Antique Buttons*, 1972, Drake Publishers, N.Y.

Peter, Mary, *Collecting Victorian Jewelry*, 1971, Emerson Books, Buchaman, N.Y.

Ross, Ishbell, *Crusades & Crinolines*, 1963, Harper & Row, New York.

Ross, Ishbell, *Silhouette in Diamonds*, first edition 1960, Harper & Brothers.

St. George, Eleanor, *The Dolls of Yesterday*, 1948, Charles Scribner's Sons.

Sage, Elizabeth, *A Study of Costume*, 1926, Charles Scribner's Sons.

Savage, George, *Glass*, 1972, Octupus Books, Ltd., London.

Schnapper, M.B., *American Labor*, 1972, Public Affairs Press, Washington, D.C.

Skinner, Cornelia Otis, *Madame Sarah*, 1967, Houghton Mifflin Company, Boston.

Van Boehn, Max, *Dolls & Puppets*, translated by Josephene Nicoll, David Mc Kay Co., Philadelphia.

Van Boehn, Max, *Modes & Manners*, translated by Joan Joshua, Vol. I-IV, 1932, J.B. Lippincott Company, Philadelphia.

Victoria and Albert Museum, *Bohemian Glass*, 1965, Her Majesty's Stationery Office.

Ware, W. Porter and Lockard, Thaddeus C., Jr., *The Lost Letters of Jenny Lind*, 1966, Victor Gollancz Ltd., London.

Webster, Robert A., *Gems: Their Sources*, Descriptions and Identification, Vol. I, 1962, Butterworth & Co., London.

Encyclopediae

Encyclopedia Americana, International Edition, Vol. XI, 1965, Americana Corporation, New York.

Encyclopedia of World Art, 1961, McGraw-Hill, selected volumes.

The New International Encyclopaedia, Selected volumes, 1907, Dodd, Mead and Company, New York.

Articles

American Heritage Magazine, Volume IX, No. 6, October 1958, p. 20-27, Hill, Ralph Nading, "Mr. Godey's Lady," American Heritage Publishing Co.

Antiques Magazine, The, August 1968, p. 220-223, Askew, Richard Burton Marlow, "Fashion Plates in America."

Atlantic Monthly, Vol. 53, 1884, p. 282-286, "Levee at the House of Worth," "Paris Dressmaker."

Blackwood's Magazine, Vol. 157, 1893, p. 79, "Worth, the Paris Dressmaker."

Harper's Monthly Magazine, March 1884, p. 518-531, "The Yorkshire Coast."

Historical New Hampshire, Vol. XXVII, No. 1, Spring 1972, p. 3-26, Ricciotti, Dominic, "Popular Art in Godey's Lady's Book," published by The New Hampshire Historical Society.

International Studio Magazine, Vol. 84, June 1926, p. 50-53, Vaughn, Malcolm, "Rare Old Spanish Carvings in Jet."

Ladies' Home Journal, Vol. 44, Feb. March April, May, 1927, Worth, Jean Phillipe, "Dressing the World of Fashion For A Century."

National Geographic Magazine, Vol. 63, Feb. 1933, p. 197-232, Wamsley, Leo, "Between the Heather and the North Sea."

Reader's Digest, April 1946, 48: 42-46, Walworth, D., "Sarah Hale and Her Lady's Book."

Scientific American, April 18, 1868, p. 243, "Cluster Work Jewelry—Report of Patent to W.O. Draper, A.C. Sweetland and G.H. Draper."

Scientific American, supplement, 51: 21072, March 16, 1901, Davenport, C., "History of Cameos."

Scientific American, No. 117, Aug. 4, 1917, p. 82, "Revival of English Jet Industry."

Periodicals:

Arthur's Magazine, 1869, selected issues.

Columbian Magazine, 1845 and 1846.

Delineator Magazine, 1890, 1891, 1893, 1896, 1906 and 1907, selected issues.

Demorest's Monthly Magazine, Jan.-Dec. 1886.

Godey's Lady's Book and Magazine, Jan. 1864-June 1864.

Graham's Magazine, Vol. 40, Jan.-Dec. 1852.

Harper's Bazar, 1879, 1880, 1881, 1883, 1884, 1885, 1894, selected issues.

Harper's Monthly Magazine, Vol. 1, 1850-Vol. 30, 1864.

Ladies' Home Journal, Issues beginning Dec. 1900-Dec. 1930.

Ladies' Own Magazine, 1873.

Frank Leslie's Magazine, New Family Magazine and Gazette of Fashion, Vol. IV, Jan. 1859-June 1859.

Frank Leslie's Monthly Magazine, Vol. X and XI, Jan. 1862-Dec. 1862.

Frank Leslie's Popular Monthly, August 1881.

Peterson's Magazine, 1887 and 1888, selected issues.

Wood's Household Magazine, 1873 and 1892, selected issues.

Young Ladies' Journal, June 1881.

———————

Catalogue of Jewelry, 1900, Robert S. Gatter Co., Century House, N.Y.

Catalogue of Lord and Taylor, Clothing and Fashions, 1881, published by The Pyne Press 1971, American Historical Catalogue Collection.

Catalogue of Marshall Fields & Co., 1896, edited by J.J. Schroeder, Jr., DBI Books, Inc., Northfield, Ill., 1970.

The Brooklyn Museum, The House of Worth, 1962.

The Wonderful World of Ladies' Fashion 1850-1920, edited by J.J. Schroeder Jr., DBI Books, Inc., Northfield, Ill., 1971.

Victorian Fashions & Costumes from Harper's Bazar 1867-1898, edited and with an introduction by Stella Blum, Dover Publications, New York, 1974.

References and Credits

2 **Photo Credits**
p. 10—Courtesy W. Porter Ware

3 **Photo Credits**
p. 12—Reprinted with permission from the Archives of Aurora College, Aurora, Illinois.

4 **References**
p. 13, 14—*The Encyclopedia Americana*, International Edition, Vol. XI, 1965, p. 51a, 51b, 51c, reprinted with permission.
p. 13,14—*Dolls & Puppets*, by Max Van Boehn, translated by Josephene Nicoll, David McKay Co., Philadelphia, Pa., p. 136, 137, 144.
p. 13, 14, 15—*Two Centuries of Costume in America*, by Alice Morse Earle, Dover Publications, Inc., New York, N.Y., p. 661, 664, 666, 745.
p. 14—*The New International Encyclopedia*, Vol. XVI, 1907, p. 691, 692, reprinted with permission of Dodd, Mead & Co., New York, N.Y.
p. 14, 15—*The History of American Costume*, by Elizabeth McClellan, Third Edition, 1937, p. 137, 138, reprinted with permission of Tudor Publishing Co. (Leon Amiel-Publisher), New York, N.Y.

Photo Credits
p. 15—Reprinted with permission of the City of Philadelphia, Department of Records, City Archives, Philadelphia, Pa.

5 **References**
p. 16—*Two Centuries of Costume in America*, by Alice Morse Earle, Dover Publications, Inc., New York, N.Y. p. 87, 87, 680.
p. 16—*The Encyclopedia Americana*, International Edition, Vol. XI, 1965, p. 51b, 51c, reprinted with permission.
p. 16—*The Encyclopedia of World Art*, Vol. 4, 1961, p. 51, 52, reprinted with permission of McGraw-Hill Book Co., New York, N.Y.
p. 17—*Fashion Through Fashion Plates*, by Doris Langley Moore, First American Edition, Clarkson N. Potter, Inc., New York, N.Y., 1971, p. 12, reprinted with permission of The Rainbird Publishing Group Limited, London, England.
p. 17—*History of American Costume*, by Elizabeth McClellan, Third Edition, 1937, p. 273, 274, reprinted with permission of Tudor Publishing Co. (Leon Amiel Publisher), New York, N.Y.
p. 17, 19, 21, 24, 26—*A History of American Magazines*, by Luther Mott, Vol. I-IV, 1957, Harvard University Press, Cambridge, Mass., p. 71, 591, 545, 547, 802, 806, 807 (Vol I); p. 557, 561, 309, 417, 418, 439, 441 (Vol. II); p. 481, 389, 574, 591 (Vol. III); p. 536 (Vol. IV); reprinted with permission.
p. 19, 26—*Godey's Lady's Book and Magazine*, 1864, p. 308, 309, 312.
p. 21, 22—*Crusades & Crinolines*, by Ishbell Ross, 1963, Harper & Row, New York, N.Y., p. 21, 22, reprinted with permission.
p. 21—*Frank Leslie's Magazine—Gazette of Fashion*, Vol. IV, March, 1859.
p. 22—*Ladies' Own Magazine*, advertisement, 1873.
p. 24—*Victorian Fashions & Costumes from Harper's Bazar*, 1867-1898, edited and with an introduction by Stella Blum, 1974, Dover Publications, New York, N.Y., reprinted with permission.

Photo Credits
Photos reprinted with permission from the Archives of Aurora College, Aurora, Illinois.

6 **References**
p. 35—*The Magazine, Antiques*, "Fashion Plates in America," by Richard Burton Marlow Askew, August, 1968, p. 220, 221, reprinted with permission.
p. 35—*The Lady of Godey's: Sarah Josepha Hale*, by Ruth E. Finley, copyright 1931 by Ruth E. Finley, copyright © renewed by the Estate of Ruth E. Finley, p. 54, reprinted by permission of J.B. Lippincott Company.
p. 35, 40—*A History of American Magazines*, by Luther Mott, Vol. I, 1957, Harvard University Press, Cambridge, Mass., p. 547, 548, 591; reprinted with permission.
p. 45—*Fashion Through Fashion Plates*, by Doris Langley Moore, First American Edition, Clarkson N. Potter, Inc., New York, N.Y., 1971, p. 17, reprinted with permission of The Rainbird Publishing Group Limited, London, England.

Photo Credits
Photos reprinted with permission from the Archives of Aurora College, Aurora, Illinois.
Photos reprinted with permission of Dover Publications, from Victorian Fashions & Costumes from *Harper's Bazar* 1867-1898, edited and with an introduction by Stella Blum, 1974.

7 **References**
p. 50—*Atlantic Monthly*, "Levee at the House of Worth," Vol. 53, 1884, p. 282.
p. 50, 57—*Blackwood's Magazine*, "Worth, the Paris Dressmaker," Vol. 157, 1893, p. 79.
p. 54—*Peterson's Magazine*, February, 1888, p. 202.
p. 54, 56—*Silhouette in Diamonds*, by Ishbell Ross, First Edition 1960, p. 169, 84, 85; reprinted with permission of Harper & Row, New York, N.Y.
p. 54—*Because I Loved Him*, by Noel Gerson, Reader's Digest Condensed Version, 1971, p. 325, 354, 377; reprinted with permission of William Morrow & Co. Publishers, Inc., New York, N.Y.
p. 54—*Eleanora Duse: The Story of Her Life*, by Jeanne Bordeux, Fifth Edition, George H. Doran Co., p. 163-168.

p. 54, 57—*Harper's Bazar*, November 5, 1881.

p. 57—*Catalogue of Lord & Taylor, Clothing and Fashions,* 1881, 1971, American Historical Catalogue Collection, p. 136, 137; reprinted with permission of the Pyne Press, Princeton, N.J.

p. 60—*Ladies' Home Journal*, "Paris, the Arbiter of Fashion," p. 79.

Photo Credits

p. 48—Courtesy of the Brooklyn Museum, New York.

Photos reprinted with permission of Dover Publications, from Victorian Fashions & Costumes from *Harper's Bazar* 1867-1898, 1974, edited and with an introduction by Stella Blum.

8 References

p. 61, 62—*Bead Embroidery*, by Joan Edwards, copyright 1966 by Joan Edwards, published by Taplinger Publishing Co., Inc., New York, p. 106, 107, 102; reprinted with permission.

p. 62, 63—*American Labor*, by M.B. Schnapper, 1972, Public Affairs Press, Washington, D.C., p. 357, 331, 80, 331, reprinted with permission.

p. 63—*Blackwood's Magazine*, "Worth, the Paris Dressmaker," Vol. 157, 1893, p. 79.

p. 63—*The Autobiography of Mother Jones*, by Mary Harris Jones, edited by Mary Field Parton, 1972, Charles H. Kerr Publishing Company, Chicago, Illinois, p. 203; reprinted with permission.

p. 63—*Silhouette in Diamonds*, by Ishbell Ross, First Edition 1960, p. 46, reprinted with permission of Harper & Row, New York, N.Y.

Photo Credits

Photos reprinted from the pages of B. Altman & Co. catalogues, by permission of the Baker Library, Harvard University, Cambridge, Mass.

Photos reprinted with permission of Dover Publications from Victorian Fashions & Costumes from *Harper's Bazar* 1867-1898, edited and with an introduction by Stella Blum, 1974.

10 References

p. 95, 96—*Two Centuries of Costume in America*, by Alice Morse Earle, Dover Publications, Inc., New York, N.Y., p. 651, 650, 657, 748.

p. 96—*The History of American Costume,* by Elizabeth McClellan, Third Edition, 1937, p. 189, 190; reprinted with permission of Tudor Publishing Co. (Leon Amiel-Publisher), New York, N.Y.

p. 99, 100—*Frank Leslie's Monthly Magazine,* 1862, p. 187, 479.

p. 103—*The Delineator,* May, 1893.

p. 103—*Ladies' Home Journal*, February, 1907, p. 64.

Photo Credits

Photo reprinted with permission of the Smithsonian Institution (photo no. 72-2416).

Photos reprinted with permission of the Archives of Aurora College, Aurora, Illinois.

Photos reprinted with permission of Dover Publications from Victorian Fashions & Costumes from *Harper's Bazar*, 1867-1898, edited and with an introduction by Stella Blum, 1974.

Photo © 1907, Curtis Publishing Co., reprinted with permission of *Ladies' Home Journal*.

12 Photo Credits

p. 109—Reprinted with permission of Charles H. Kerr Publishing Company, from *The Autobiography of Mother Jones,* edited by Mary Field Parton, 1972.

13 References

p. 110—*A Glossary of Minerology*, by Henry Bristow, 1861, Longman, Green, Longman and Roberts, London, p. 197.

p. 110, 113—*National Geographic Magazine,* "Between the Heather and the North Sea," by Leo Wamsley, Vol. 63, February, 1933, p. 202, 215, 216; reprinted with permission.

p. 110, 111—*Harper's Monthly Magazine*, "The Yorkshire Coast," March, 1884, p. 519, 525; 522.

p. 111—*International Studio Magazine*, "Rare Old Spanish Carvings in Jet," by Malcolm Vaughn, Vol. 84, June, 1926, p. 50-53.

p. 111—*Les Miserables*, by Victor Hugo, translated by Lascelles Wraxall, Heritage Press, 1938, reprinted with permission.

p. 112—*Collecting Victorian Jewelry*, by Mary Peter, 1971, Emerson Books, Reynolds Lane, Buchanan, N.Y., p. 76, reprinted with permission.

p. 112—113—*Old Glass*, by N.H. Moore, copyright 1924 by Frederick A. Stokes Company, copyright 1924 by J.B. Lippincott Company, copyright renewed 1952 by Edmund W. Moore, p. 49, 50, 59; reprinted with permission.

p. 112—*Demorest's Monthly Magazine*, Spring and Summer Semi-Annual Book, 1874.

p. 113—*Scientific American*, "Revival of English Jet Industry," No. 117, August 4, 1917, p. 82, reprinted with permission.

Photo Credits

p. 112—Reprinted with permission of the Aurora Historical Society, Aurora, Illinois.

14 References

p. 118—*Bead Embroidery*, by Joan Edwards, copyright 1966 by Joan Edwards, published by Taplinger Publishing Co., Inc., New York, p. 23, 24, 25, 26, 28; reprinted with permission.

p. 118, 120—*Collecting Antique Jewelry,* by Mona Curran, Second Edition 1970, Emerson Books, Buchanan, N.Y., p. 81, 80, 85; reprinted with permission.

p. 123—*The Button Collector's History*, by Grace Horney Ford, 1943, Pond Ekberg Co., Springfield, Mass. (to be republished by the New England Publishing Co., Stratford, Conn.), p. 123, 124, reprinted with permission.

p. 126, 128—*Collecting Victorian Jewelry*, by Mary Peter, 1971, Emerson Books, Reynolds Lane, Buchanan, N.Y., p. 57, 52, reprinted with permission.

p. 136—*Button Guide*, by American Life Foundation, Books 1 and 2, 1972, American Life Foundation, Watkins Glen, N.Y. (distributed by Century House Inc.., Watkins Glen, N.Y.), p. 52 (Book 2), reprinted with permission.

p. 136—*Antique Buttons*, by Primrose Peacock, 1972, Drake Publishers, N.Y., p. 49, reprinted with permission.

Photo Credits

Photo reprinted with permission of Mackinac Island State Park Commission from Fort Michilimackinac 1717-1781.

Photos reprinted from pages of the B. Altman & Co. catalogues with permission of the Baker Library, Harvard University, Cambridge, Mass.

Photos reprinted from the 1896 Marshall Field & Co. jewelry catalogue with permission of DBI Books, Inc., Northfield, Illinois.

Photos reprinted with permission of Aurora College, Aurora, Illinois.

Photos reprinted with permission of Dover Publications from Victorian Fashions & Costumes from *Harper's Bazar* 1867-1898, edited and with an introduction by Stella Blum, 1974.

Sketches from the pages of the *Ladies' Home Journal* drawn with permission from Downe Publishing Company.

15 Photo Credits

Photo of the horn book reprinted with permission of Aurora College, Aurora, Illinois.

Index